Manfred Bortenschlager

The Concept of Coordination

How to Exploit an Optimization Potential

Südwestdeutscher Verlag für Hochschulschriften

Impressum/Imprint (nur für Deutschland/ only for Germany)
Bibliografische Information der Deutschen Nationalbibliothek: Die Deutsche Nationalbibliothek verzeichnet diese Publikation in der Deutschen Nationalbibliografie; detaillierte bibliografische Daten sind im Internet über http://dnb.d-nb.de abrufbar.
Alle in diesem Buch genannten Marken und Produktnamen unterliegen warenzeichen-, markenoder patentrechtlichem Schutz bzw. sind Warenzeichen oder eingetragene Warenzeichen der jeweiligen Inhaber. Die Wiedergabe von Marken, Produktnamen, Gebrauchsnamen, Handelsnamen, Warenbezeichnungen u.s.w. in diesem Werk berechtigt auch ohne besondere Kennzeichnung nicht zu der Annahme, dass solche Namen im Sinne der Warenzeichen- und Markenschutzgesetzgebung als frei zu betrachten wären und daher von jedermann benutzt werden dürften.

Verlag: Südwestdeutscher Verlag für Hochschulschriften Aktiengesellschaft & Co. KG
Dudweiler Landstr. 99, 66123 Saarbrücken, Deutschland
Telefon +49 681 37 20 271-1, Telefax +49 681 37 20 271-0, Email: info@svh-verlag.de
Zugl.: Linz, Johannes Kepler Universität, Dissertation, 2008

Herstellung in Deutschland:
Schaltungsdienst Lange o.H.G., Berlin
Books on Demand GmbH, Norderstedt
Reha GmbH, Saarbrücken
Amazon Distribution GmbH, Leipzig
ISBN: 978-3-8381-0357-0

Imprint (only for USA, GB)
Bibliographic information published by the Deutsche Nationalbibliothek: The Deutsche Nationalbibliothek lists this publication in the Deutsche Nationalbibliografie; detailed bibliographic data are available in the Internet at http://dnb.d-nb.de.
Any brand names and product names mentioned in this book are subject to trademark, brand or patent protection and are trademarks or registered trademarks of their respective holders. The use of brand names, product names, common names, trade names, product descriptions etc. even without a particular marking in this works is in no way to be construed to mean that such names may be regarded as unrestricted in respect of trademark and brand protection legislation and could thus be used by anyone.

Publisher:
Südwestdeutscher Verlag für Hochschulschriften Aktiengesellschaft & Co. KG
Dudweiler Landstr. 99, 66123 Saarbrücken, Germany
Phone +49 681 37 20 271-1, Fax +49 681 37 20 271-0, Email: info@svh-verlag.de

Copyright © 2009 by the author and Südwestdeutscher Verlag für Hochschulschriften Aktiengesellschaft & Co. KG and licensors
All rights reserved. Saarbrücken 2009

Printed in the U.S.A.
Printed in the U.K. by (see last page)
ISBN: 978-3-8381-0357-0

To Natasha

Preface

This book is about the concept of coordination, which can be adopted to exploit an optimisation potential in various forms. For this, it is necessary to make the concept explicit and to understand it. I try to explain coordination in a general way. The concept itself is domain independent anyway. In order to understand it better I adopt coordination to the domain of mobile collaboration and show the optimisation potential.

This book contains parts of my Computer Science PhD thesis but in a more general way. I elaborated the PhD contents further and tried to make them better understandable also for a broader public. The original PhD thesis can be obtained by contacting me[1].

In the PhD thesis, I answered the question (hypothesis) whether an explicit consideration of coordination theory in the engineering of systems for collaboration support in pervasive environments can improve the effectiveness and efficiency of mobile users. For this, I investigated several research questions and implemented an IT based system that exploits coordination theory. The hypothesis could be verified.

This book presents the results of the work conducted during the PhD thesis but goes beyond these subjects. I try to present coordination on a broader and more general perspective and deviate from a purely technical point of view.

Thanks go to my PhD supervisors Gabriele Kotsis and Sigi Reich but also to Franco Zambonelli and John Nealon, who accompanied parts of my way along the PhD program. In particular, I also would like to thank Natasha for her understanding, availability, and love. To her I dedicate this book.

Salzburg, April 2009   *Manfred Bortenschlager*

---

[1] Contact e-mail: `manfred.bortenschlager@gmx.at`

Contents

1	**The Objective of this Book**	**1**
2	**What is Coordination ?**	**3**
	2.1 Classifications and Types of Coordination	3
	2.2 The Interdisciplinary Study of Coordination	7
	2.3 Chapter Summary	9
3	**Harnessing Coordination for Collaboration**	**11**
	3.1 Mobile Collaboration	13
	3.1.1 Pervasive Computing Environments	13
	3.1.2 Emergency Management	18
	3.2 CorA – A Coordination Architecture for Pervasive Environments	21
	3.2.1 The CorA System Design	21
	3.2.2 A Formalization of CorA	49
	3.3 Coordination Language Implementation	63
	3.3.1 System Use Case Descriptions	64
	3.3.2 Components and Classes	71
	3.3.3 CorA's Internal Logics	80
	3.3.4 Application Programming Interface	87
	3.4 Chapter Summary	90
4	**Evaluation of the Optimisation Potential in Collaboration**	**93**
	4.1 Evaluation on System-Level	93
	4.1.1 Test Strategy	94
	4.1.2 Test Set-up	94
	4.1.3 Test Results	96
	4.1.4 Replication Cost Analysis	101
	4.2 Evaluation on Developer-Level	102
	4.2.1 Introduction to WORKPAD	102
	4.2.2 The WORKPAD System Architecture	103
	4.2.3 The Adoption of CorA in WORKPAD	104
	4.2.4 Exploitation of the GIS Application	105
	4.3 Evaluation on User-Level	109
	4.4 Related Work	110

		4.4.1 Coordination in Other Disciplines	111
		4.4.2 Tuple Spaces	112
		4.4.3 Software Agents	117
		4.4.4 Other Related Topics	119
	4.5	Interpretation and Reflection	121
	4.6	Chapter Summary	124

5 Coordination and Beyond — 127

Appendix — 129

Definitions 129

Chapter 1

The Objective of this Book

The term *coordination* is omnipresent and people usually have a very good understand what it actually stands for. It is difficult to explain explicitly, though. We recognise, for instance, if something is organised or *coordinated* in an ineffective way by observing the negative effects such as spending unnecessary extra resources—such as time or money. If we manage to tackle problems by focusing on coordination we might be able to resolve problems in a more efficient way. But to do so we need to understand the concept of coordination better and make it explicit in our comprehension. This, in fact, is what we would like to accomplish with this book.

As an initial food for thought, coordination is basically the way how interdependencies that are naturally occurring during processes or problems are resolved. The better they are resolved the less effort is needed to accomplish a process or to solve a problem. Hence, by trying to improve this management of interdependencies we can *optimise* our activities—and this is true for all domains as the concept of coordination is interdisciplinary and orthogonal. In other words, the management of interdependencies hides an *optimisation potential* that shall not be unexplored. Aristole claimed that each human being is a "zoon politikon" who by nature is social and tries to arrange within a community with other individuals in order to collectively gain mutual benefit. In a way, we strive for continuous optimisation of our lives and activities. We claim that explicitly looking at and understanding the concepts of coordination can be one approach to optimisation.

In this book, we first start with explaining coordination, classifying it, and giving details about the formal coordination theory. In order to make the concepts more tangible we explain it by applying them to a concrete domain. The domain is collaboration in particular of users who are mobile and work together in teams. This is a good an representative example of coordination that helps to make the concepts clearer. We call this *mobile collaboration*. We present an IT[1] based system that shall help to gain benefits from exploiting coordination theory. We give details about the system implementation and the adoption to a concrete showcase of mobile collaboration, which is part of an emergency management system that helps coordinating mobile operators on field. This showcase helps to exemplify the optimisation potential that lies in addressing coordination. We conclude the book with evaluating this approach and with an outlook about novel (IT) technologies that could further help to harness the optimisation potential of coordination.

---

[1] IT stands for Information Technology.

Chapter 2

What is Coordination ?

"Coordination" is derived from the Latin[1] verb "ordinare" which means "to arrange" or "to organize", and "co" stands for "together". So, coordination literally means that something needs to be arranged among several entities. Consequently, coordination is a rather abstract concept that is omnipresent and can be observed in many different situations and cases. In this Chapter, we first give an overview of various different classifications and types of coordination. In the second part we give an introduction to the formal theory of coordination and define this concept for our purposes.

2.1 Classifications and Types of Coordination

In general, it can be differentiated between *individual* and *collective* coordination. Collective coordination refers to coordination between several individuals or actors, respectively, such as human beings, software agents, or robots. Individual coordination, in contrast, refers to coordination related to only one such individual and describes the act of coordinating this individual's task, potentially involved constraints, and its interaction with the environment, into which the individual is embedded, such as for example necessary resources.

A classical individual coordination example was described by Social Psychologist Kurt Lewin in 1935: the so called "approach-avoidance conflict" [105], which represents a contribution to Motivation Psychology. This conflict denotes the case when an individual has to decide between a goal—and the involved activities—that is necessary but is unpleasant and a goal that is pleasant but not necessary and contradicting the other goal. As an example consider a student who has to attend an exam the next day, which requires studying in the afternoon and evening, or a BBQ event, which involves shopping and preparation. Either the student has to decide for one of the two goal options or she manages to ideally *coordinate* her activities in order to be able to attend both (with the danger of failing in both: fail the exam due to insufficient preparation and not amusing herself during the BBQ due to her bad conscience and not being relaxed).

There is an large number of such examples. Another one would be in work-life. This is an example of collective coordination. Consider a project manager. In order to achieve his goals in time, in budget, and with the required quality (i.e., the outcome meets the customers' expectations) he needs to coordinate a lot of activities, actors, and resources. First, the project goals need to be clear and quantified. Then, the project manager needs to break the work down into work packages and related activities which are inter-dependent among each other. He has to define a timeline, identify the critical path, and make sure that the necessary

---
[1] See, for instance, Stowasser's Latin dictionary.

resources are available when needed. In other words, he has to coordinate inter-dependent activities, the involved actors, and has to consider various types of constraints—such as temporal, spatial, or causal constraints or constraints related to available resources.

Coordination apparently is omnipresent and plays a vital role in many different domains and disciplines such as social sciences, politics, psychology, sociology, economics, finance, anthropology, biology, management theories, organization theories, operations management, logistics or computer science. What the entries of this incomplete list have in common is the fact that coordination is used to achieve something greater such as optimisation, which shall lead to savings in resources such as time or money and, finally, lead to wealth and prosperity. Also an increase in health and safety represents a motivation for several entities to coordinate. As also already stated by Aristotle, human beings are by nature social and community building creatures—the "zoon politikon"—and mutual arrangements to achieve more than an individual would ever be able to achieve are a human want [88].

In particular in sociology the term "coordination problem" defines the fact that a problem does not necessarily have an objectively correct solution but which is framed in terms of coordinating actions with everyone else's actions [163]. Driving on a freeway requires that one's speed and actions needs to be coordinated with those of other drivers. In order to determine the fastest route to work in traffic also the time of day needs to be coordinated—indirectly in this case—to avoid getting stuck. Groups are not guaranteed to come up with optimal solutions but often do, which is referred to as "collective intelligence". Another example discussed by Surowiecki in his seminal work [163] for a coordination problem that is difficult to solve is the fact that a bar should be full with people up to 60%. Way below that level is too few people, hence, boring; way beyond is too many, hence, too crowded. The difficulty for a single visitor is to estimate the level, which can possibly be derived from related facts such as weather.

In economy, markets are a prototypical example of coordination problems. Prices are defined by sellers (supply) and buyers (demand) through some way of coordination. Game theory—developed by von Neumann and Morgenstern [178]—is the discipline that mainly deals with coordination problems not only in economics but also in other social sciences, political science, biology, engineering, computer science (mainly for artificial intelligence), and philosophy [65]. In game theory, coordination problems are formalized as "coordination games". Coordination games describe situations in which all parties can realize mutual benefits but only by making mutually consistent decisions, which requires coordination. An example is driving on the same side of the road which is defined as a social standard. Likewise is the adoption of technology standards in industry. The example of driving on the correct side of the road is a two-player, two-strategy coordination game[2] also referred to as coordination game with two Nash equilibria. A Nash equilibrium describes a solution which was chosen because all involved parties could gain mutual benefit by changing their strategy [124]. This example has two Nash equilibria because both can either choose to drive on the right or on the left side. Only the same decision, however, leads to mutual benefit (i.e., no crash) and, hence, to a Nash equilibrium. The pure coordination game is thus Pareto optimal[3]. Other examples of such mathematically formalized games, which are applied to social sciences or economics, are the pure (or common interest) coordination game (the Nash equilibria are not equally preferable), conflicting interest coordination game (not all strategies are equally beneficial for all players), competition game (players need to choose a better strategy as the opponent), stag hunt game (players only benefit if they cooperate; anyone, however, has attractive alternatives), or prisoner's dilemma (there is only one Nash equilibrium).

---

[2]This can be extended to an n-player, m-strategy coordination game.
[3]Further Pareto improvements would not improve the situation of any player.

Coordination problems can appear in many different facets and can be solved in many different ways. One such solution is central control or planning. This involves one omniscient authority that possesses the global knowledge and coordinates the activities of other entities. This is, however, often not possible, feasible, or desirable. The contrary is that all involved entities are equal and possess all the necessary coordination knowledge themselves.

This differentiation between authoritarian control or autonomy in coordination decision also corresponds to centralised or decentralised organization of entities. In ICT, a classic example of a centralised organization are client/server (C/S) based systems such as the World Wide Web. The distribution (i.e., coordination) of information is done by clients requesting data from central servers. Usually, clients outnumber servers by far and the role of the client is always the service consumer where the server is always the service provider. This architectural approach suffices for a magnitude of situations and applications. In some cases, however, this type suffers from severe drawbacks. Due to the centralised design, servers may not be able to respond to too large number of client requests. Moreover, a server represents a single point of failure and may be subject to attacks from malicious individuals. Due to the fact that resources are solely provided by the server, its unavailability is going to result in unavailability of the whole service or system, respectively, leading to uselessness.

In contrast, a different and decentralised architectural approach is termed as peer-to-peer (P2P) networks. A peer-to-peer system refers to a distributed network of interconnected, heterogeneous entities (peers) which are able to dynamically adapt to the topology of the overlay network defined by the available nodes, for the purpose of exploiting shared resources respectively distributed information independent from any central authority, where communication is conducted in an equal way among equal nodes; where each node has an equal right to transiently adopt a certain role (see also Definition 10). The decentralised nature of such networks offers the avoidance of any single points of failure. Also due to this "decentralism", robustness, availability and fault-tolerance can be significantly increased through replication and redundant storage of data [3]. Also, C/S systems may behave too static in pervasive environments. P2P systems, however, are able to address frequent changes more flexible and thus seem to be more appropriate in such situations [97]. Because of their inherent adaptability, such networks are very well prepared to address such frequent changes due to a great autonomy of the involved nodes resulting in a self-regulating behaviour [52].

A further interesting phenomenon which is closely related to decentralised systems is the *small world* effect [116]. In 1967, social scientist Stanley Milgram conducted an experiment where he asked 160 randomly chosen people (from Omaha, Nebraska) to pass a certain letter to a specific person (in Boston, Massachusetts) by handing this letter only to a person personally known by them, and of who they thought would bring the letter closer to the target person. 42 letters really reached this person and just a median of 5.5 intermediary people were needed for doing that. Subsequently, mathematicians were able to mathematically reproduce and prove this concept. On average, six relations are necessary to reach any node in such a small world network, which is also referred to as the *six degrees of separation* phenomenon [116]. Milgram also discovered, that many letters independently went similar paths indicating the presence of so called super-nodes or bridges. In graph theory and network research, networks containing such super-nodes are called scale-free networks where a minority of the nodes exhibit a unproportionally large number of links to other nodes, which follows a power-law degree distribution. The benefit of such networks—which are a type of P2P networks—is their scalability and adaptability feature through their self-regulating behaviour. Due to the high degree of connectedness, information or messages can be distributed through the whole network very quickly. Furthermore, such networks offer a high resilience to accidental failures because the probability to remove a less important node is high. Examples of such networks are the routing mechanisms behind the Internet, all kinds of social networks between human beings (including collaboration networks), the power supply system, or the references between scientific papers [8].

A classification can also be done according to direct or indirect coordination. In the direct interaction mode, entities interact in a direct and explicit way among each other. The other possibility of interaction is indirect interaction for example via the environment or by conventions or rules. In order to achieve the overall goal, the necessary indirect communication is conducted by sensing the local environment, modifying it accordingly, and by reacting to changes. In other words, an entity's actions leaves signs in the environment, signs that it and other entities are able to sense and that determine their subsequent actions. The earlier coordination problem of determining the best route to work in traffic is an example for indirect coordination with the traffic environment and other participants. This concept is also referred to as *stigmergy* [74, 83], which is derived from the Greek words stigma (=sign) and ergon (=action) and was first observed in nature. Stigmergy is defined as a paradigm of indirect and asynchronous communication mediated by the environment [57]. Ants, for instance, follow trails of pheromones produced by other ants in order to guide each other. Hence, this aspect of an ant colony is a stigmergic system where ants communicate via the environment by laying down pheromones. Stigmergy is also relevant in technical systems such as the Internet when users produce a certain trail of navigation which can be exploited for other users with similar intentions [68].

The concept behind Brook's subsumption architecture [26] is based on very similar ideas. It is a concept originating from behaviour based robotics out of artificial intelligence (AI) research. The idea is to decompose complex behaviours into many simple layers, each built on top of the ones beneath it and each comprising more abstract behaviours. A topmost layer could be "create a map" representing the overall goal. The following layers are "explore the world", "wander around", and the lowest "avoid an object". One layer can *subsume* its underlying layer(s). This way, the lowest layers can work like fast-adapting mechanisms such as reflexes, while the higher layers control the main direction to be taken in order to achieve the overall goal. Feedback is given mainly through the environment. Brooks developed a six-legged robot based on the subsumption architecture, where each leg autonomously scanned the environment and acted on it directly in pursuit of its own agenda. By scanning and acting, and trial and error a walking behaviour of the robot finally emerged.

In some cases, cultural references or conventions help us in solving coordination problems indirectly. Experiments [149] showed that people managed to coordinate without any communication at all only by exploiting well-known reference points—so called Schelling or focal points. Schelling showed that a majority of people responded when they where asked where to meet a stranger in New York at noon under the big clock of the Central Station[4].

As mentioned earlier, another typology of coordination is individual versus collective. Also, it can be differentiated between intentional versus unintentional (entities either need to coordinate explicitly or coordination is merely an effect of a certain activity), competitive versus cooperative (entities are either in a competitive or in a cooperative relationship), or coordination can be conducted a priori defined (according to a plan) or determined and executed in an ad hoc manner according to the current context.

To summarize, coordination as a concept is quite abstract and inter- and multidisciplinary. Nevertheless, people have a good intuitive notion about what coordination actually means. It penetrates our daily lives and is omnipresent. It mostly becomes apparent when it is lacking or badly "implemented". The same or similar coordination strategies or mechanisms can be applied to very diverse disciplines [109]. The principal task of coordination is to jointly achieve a common, superior goal as effectively, fast, and economically as possible by integrating and adjusting individual work efforts harmoniously [159].

---

[4]Schelling points are an integral part of the developed coordination architecture (see Section 3.2.1.5 on page 39).

2.2 The Interdisciplinary Study of Coordination

The formal and interdisciplinary study of coordination (i.e., coordination theory) [109] tries to tackle the coordination issue and to formalize its abstract concepts. Malone and Crowston used a formal approach to describe coordination theory as an interdisciplinary subject which comprises four coordination entities [109]: goals, activities, actors, and interdependencies. In that work, a definition of coordination is given as:

> Coordination is the act of managing interdependencies between activities.

Consequently, the challenge is to investigate and to elaborate accordant mechanisms to resolve the interdependencies, which is the key to improve coordination. To accomplish this, coordination laws are established and applied defining *how* to resolve the interdependencies.

In this work, we recognised the need for amending the aforementioned approach of Malone and Crowston to be comprised now of five coordination entities, which we considered as more accurate:

1. *Goals:* This is what should be achieved through the coordination process.

2. *Actors:* They are the executing entities in such a process.

3. *Activities:* These are the tasks that need to be done in order to achieve goals.

4. *Constraints:* The other coordination entities can be constrained by several facts such as temporal, spatial, or causal aspects.

5. *Interdependencies:* All coordination entities are interdependent among and within each other.

This extension to the original model of Malone and Crowston also led us to extend the definition of "coordination":

> Coordination is the act of managing *interdependencies* between *actors* and *activities* by consideration of *constraints* for the purpose of achieving *goals*.

This definition is used in this work[5]. With this model (definition plus the five entities) we argue to have the means of breaking down and better understanding coordination problems, which is the prerequisite of developing a solution. In the model, the main strategy to solve coordination problems or to improve such solutions is the focus on resolving interdependencies in various forms [109].

Human beings naturally try to continuously optimise; in the sense that processes or activities in daily live should be accomplished more efficient and effective in order to save time and money and to increase quality. Coordination exhibits an optimisation potential. When we succeed in improving the way interdependencies are resolved activities in a process can be executed in an improved way, thus leading to the desired savings. By focusing and improving coordination we *optimise*. An interesting example comes from project management—in this case of information technology (IT) projects. Alistair Cockburn describes in his book about agile software development [42] that in particular among the members of a project team a lot of communication and coordination is necessary. The larger, more complex a project is and the more people are involved, the more interdependencies emerge and the higher is the demand for coordination. If a project for any reason is late and results cannot delivered the obvious remedy would be to add more members. This, however, is a fallacy

---

[5]See Definition 3.

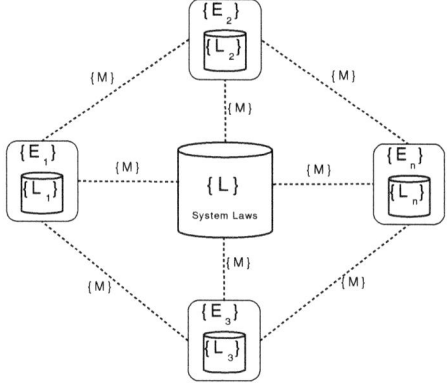

Figure 2.1: Ciancarini's Coordination Triple {E, M, L} [40]

as adding more staff to a late project makes it even later. This phenomenon was also discovered earlier as the "mythical man-month" by Frederick P. Brooks in [25]. Adding more people implicates that the coordination efforts increase, too, i.e. more interdependencies to manage. The new people require more and additional meetings and trainings preventing the original project staff from working on the project. The better solution is to keep the size of the team and ask the people to work overtime. The more clever solution for a project manager is to try hard that such a situation does not arise at all by paying close attention to managing the interdependencies between actors and (temporal) constraints in particular, which is easier said than done.

In computer science, many efforts have to be invested in defining appropriate mechanisms. In order to accomplish this, usually coordination laws are established and applied. Ciancarini states that such laws are a necessary part of any coordinative process [40]. To described this, he formulated the coordination triple of {E, M, L}. In this generic model, {E} represents the coordinable (either physical or logical) entities which have to be coordinated. These can be (software) processes, services, (software) agents, or even human beings interacting with computer-based systems. {M} stands for the coordination media (i.e. communication channels), which serve as connectors between the entities and facilitate communication, which is a mandatory prerequisite for intentional and direct coordination [40]. Instances of coordination media may be a message-passing environment, pipes, remote-procedure calls, or shared spaces [110]. {L} is referred to the coordination laws defining how the interdependencies which are the focal point in coordination have to be resolved and hence, semantically define the coordination mechanisms. Figure 2.1 illustrates a variant of this {E, M, L} model. It can basically be differentiated between system wide coordination laws {L} which can be accessed and are known by every coordinable {E_i}. In addition, every coordinable controls its own coordination laws {L_i}, with which local coordination problems (e.g., referring to individual coordination) can be resolved. The communication between all entities is facilitated through coordination media {M} indicated by dotted lines in Figure 2.1.

Another coordination model originally proposed in the context of computer science was introduced by Klein in [100]. This so called 3C model (communication, coordination, collaboration) was discovered and adopted in the domain of human collaboration. Klein correlates communication, coordination, and collaboration and argues that communication is necessary for coordination which improves collaboration and by this, communication enables collaboration. A more detailed discussion on the 3C model can be found in Section 3 (see Figure 3.1 on page 12).

In this book, we use coordination theory and related models as introduced here as vehicles to better understand the concepts behind problems and to show the possible optimisation in the field of computer science. We use a particular sub-domain for showcasing how coordination can be exploited. This sub-domain is collaboration of mobile users, which is referred to as *mobile collaboration*. As a concrete showcase we adopt the mechanisms in mobile collaboration applications for emergency management scenarios.

2.3 Chapter Summary

In this Chapter we gave general information about coordination. The first Section contained a broader discussion on the concept of coordination in general terms. We differentiated between various facets of coordination such as individual versus collective, centralised versus decentralised, authoritarian control versus autonomy, direct versus indirect, intentional versus unintentional, competitive versus cooperative, or a priori defined versus ad hoc executed. Moreover, we presented coordination as it is used in other disciplines such as social sciences (e.g., collective intelligence, Schelling points), economy (Game Theory and coordination games), and computer science.

In the second Section we introduced coordination theory and gave the original definition and our adapted definition. We also discussed the five coordination entities (goals, actors, activities, constraints, and interdependencies) to which we will refer back throughout the book. We presented Ciancarini's coordination triple {E, M, L} and Klein's 3C model as representative coordination models from the computer science domain and gave examples of coordination from project management.

The following Chapter presents how we embodied the theory of coordination in an IT based system and exploited it for collaboration of mobile users in pervasive environments.

Chapter 3

Harnessing Coordination for Collaboration

The motivation of this book is to highlight the fact that explicitly dealing with coordination can lead to optimisation. In order to exemplify this we would like to adopt the concepts to a concrete example in the domain of *collaboration*.

The widespread use of information and communication technologies (ICT), computers, and networks of computers entailed the exploitation of such technologies for collaboration. ICT can represent an added-value to (distributed) collaboration and, in fact, can enable ways of distributed working which would not be able without. In the previous Chapter 2 we already introduced the interrelation between coordination and collaboration (see page 9).

In Computer Science, the theoretical foundations and methodologies for teamwork and its support through computers is subsumed by the *Computer Supported Cooperative Work* (CSCW) discipline [12]. Wilson defines CSCW as "a generic term which combines the understanding of the way people work in groups with the enabling technologies of computer networking, and associated hardware, software, services and techniques" [184].

To better understand the scope, it is interesting to analyse the expression *Computer Supported Cooperative Work* word by word in a backward way [12].

Work is the central issue of CSCW. A particular work activity, which usually can be separated into various tasks, needs to be accomplished. It can also be considered as a value chain system that shall produce an output that is more valuable than the original inputs. Several components are necessary for this like the necessary working steps or tasks, actors processing these tasks, and resources that can be exploited.

Cooperative work is what we refer to as collaboration in this book and Definition 1 on page 129). Unfortunately, when the term Computer Supported Cooperative Work was first coined by Irene Greif and Paul Cashman in 1984 during a small workshop in Massachusetts, USA, that brought together various people from different fields who were interested in using technology to support people in their work, the term was used inaccurately. Today, it is commonly agreed that collaboration is the closer form of working together. While cooperation merely means to work jointly for mutual benefit, collaboration means cooperation but additionally with the same joint goal[1]. Today, referring to "cooperative work" with the C and W in CSCW is an established expression. We decided, however, to use the more accurate term "collaboration" throughout the book. By

---

[1] See the Merriam-Webster Online Dictionary at http://www.merriam-webster.com.

11

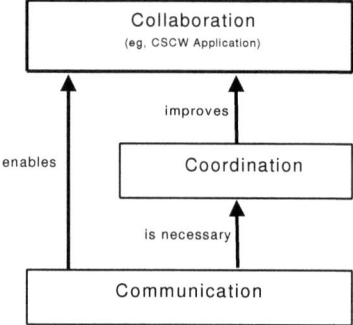

Figure 3.1: Relation between Communication, Coordination, and Collaboration

collaboration, of actors a common goal can be reached more easily, quickly, effectively and efficiently. The basis for collaboration is communication [168]. Collaboration can be classified according to the intensity and intention of communication [7]. The lowest level of communication is the mere exchange of information. More communication is necessary for coordination of either information or activities between entities. The highest level is represented by communication for collaboration, where the participants strive for a common goal.

Also Klein states that collaboration is based on communication [100]. He argues that communication is necessary for coordination which improves collaboration and by this, communication enables collaboration. Figure 3.1 illustrates the inter-relation and is adapted from [100]. The model of communication intensity described in [7] can be mapped to Klein's model as the necessary level of communication also increases with the intention. The intensity is less if it is only intended for information distribution (bottom block in Figure 3.1) and it is more if it is intended for collaboration (top block in Figure 3.1).

Supported cooperative work generally refers to any support system that assists the involved participants in their work completion. This can subsume methods, techniques, or tools such as for example collective brainstorming or brainwriting, distributed mind-mapping, Ishikawa diagrams (or cause-and-effect diagram), or force field analysis. Basically, it distinguishes between support on a data or content level (i.e., the information that is produced, processed, and exploited by the participants) and support on a process level (i.e., improving the workflow).

Computer supported cooperative work, finally, denotes that computer based systems and concepts from computer science are used to support collaboration. A common way of conceptualizing CSCW systems is to consider the context of a system's use. One such taxonomy was proposed in [77] which considers work contexts along two dimensions: space and time. It differentiated whether collaboration is co-located or geographically distributed, and whether individuals collaborate synchronously or asynchronously. It is further distinguished between predictability or unpredictability with respect to either space or time. This adds up to a 3x3 matrix as illustrated in Table 3.1, which gives several examples for CSCW systems according to each type.

The most interesting sectors where ICT can contribute the most and, thus, achieve the greatest effects are those where participants are geographically separated (these are the rows at the bottom in Figure 3.1 in

		Time		
		Synchronous	Asynchronous	
			Predictable	Unpredictable
Space	Co-located	Face-to-Face Meeting	Work Shifts	Team Meeting Rooms
	Remote Predictable	Tele-Conference	E-mail	Collaborative Writing
	Remote Unpredictable	Mobile Phone Conference	Online Bulletin Boards	Workflow Management

Table 3.1: CSCW Taxonomy [77]

italic font). These sectors are addressed by the research area called *Telecooperation*. Telecooperation investigates theories, concepts, and means that target at collaboration among human beings and machines, based on information and communication technology where these participants are spatially distributed[2].

The prime focus of this research work is *mobile* collaboration which is a particular instance and a subset of collaboration. As the collaborating entities (e.g., human users) are mobile and operating in pervasive environments, this type of collaboration systems essentially represent an example of spatial distribution where the participant's location usually is not predictable. The time of interaction is mostly unpredictable, too.

3.1 Mobile Collaboration

The challenge of systems addressing mobile collaboration scenarios is to provide "a rich set of capabilities and services to the [user] as he/she moves from place to place in a transparent and convenient form" [101, p.46]. In other words, such systems should embody transparent virtual networks that shall permit users and programs to be as effective as possible in an environment of steadily uncertain connectivity (such as pervasive environments), without significant changes of the manner in which they are used to operate. This shall be accomplished through transparent adaptations, which is the ability to automatically adjust the networking, storage, processing, and interfacing methods according to the changing environments in such a way that the user is not significantly obstructed in his activities. Hence, mobile collaboration is about managing steady changes and dynamics. A very typical application area is emergency management which is introduced in detail later in Section 3.1.2.

Mobile collaboration scenarios are inherently coupled with pervasive environments. In fact, they are embedded in pervasive environments. Mobile users can only exploit services if they address the specific characteristics and requirements of pervasive environments. Both together is labelled as a pervasive information system. The following Section (Section 3.1.1) introduces this type of information system.

3.1.1 Pervasive Computing Environments

With *pervasive computing environments* we denote environments in which users can be supported by information systems in an anytime, anywhere and anyhow fashion. As claimed by Mahadev Satyanarayanan in [146]

---
[2]This definition of Telecooperation stems from the works of Max Mühlhäuser. See http://www.tk.informatik.tu-darmstadt.de/

this support must be unobtrusive and must not hamper users' activities. In contrast to stationary environments like at home or in the office, mobility is inherent to pervasive environments, which results in different requirements and new challenges for pervasive computing system developers. Before going into details about the characteristics of pervasive environments we would like to briefly recap the evolution towards pervasive information systems.

Vannevar Bush's vision about the Memory Extender (Memex) described in his seminal work "As We May Think" [28] became reality with personal desktop computers, which can be used by individuals for storing "all his books, records, and communications" and, thus, represents "an enlarged intimate supplement to his memory". The functionality and usefulness of these personal appliances was even increased by connecting them through a network. Which is what we have in the form of the Internet which provides rich services such as the World Wide Web exploiting hypertext technology (which was also inspired by Bush's work) or e-mail.

With today's technologies and possibilities we can even go one step further. Recent developments and technological advances in information and communication technology are leading to an increasing availability and functionality of mobile and portable devices and an improved quality-of-service of wireless connections together with decreasing costs [113]. The Internet and (mobile) telecommunication networks are currently converging to one vast and ubiquitously available information space. With these, we can now move from static and stationary environments (such as home or office) to dynamic environments serving users while being mobile by portable computers in various forms. Such environments are subsumed as *pervasive environments*. The current trends and evolving technologies shall be exploited to beneficially assist the users' in their daily activities—but as unobtrusively as possible. This is the major claim and challenge at the same time of pervasive computing [146] which is the scientific discipline that aims at realising pervasive environments. Mark Weiser described this most accurately in his article [181] as "the most profound technologies are those that [...] weave themselves into the fabric of everyday life until they are indistinguishable from it". People and their activities— in particular collaborative activities in the scope of this work—shall be *supported* by using pervasive computing technology that is invisible or ambient. The magnitude and diversity of computing entities involved in pervasive environments are increasing, where at the same time these entities are miniaturised. Not only computers and embedded devices (such as sensors) are equipped with computational capabilities but also everyday objects such as clothes, which is subsumed as wearable computing [141, 169].We are moving towards the *Internet of Things* [73] and we are shifting from the *one person is associated with one computer paradigm* to a one-to-numerous relationship. *Things* can be equipped with the necessary computational and network means in order to be integrated into pervasive information systems. These things—in principle independent of their nature—can now serve human beings in supporting our activities in daily lives.

Pervasive computing is often equated with *ubiquitous computing*. Mark Weiser defines ubiquitous computing as "the method of enhancing computer use by making many computers available throughout the physical environment, but making them effectively invisible to the user" [182]. IBM's definition of pervasive computing describes the "convenient access, through a new class of appliances, to relevant information with the ability to easily take action on it when and where you need it" [79], which in essence yields a similar proposition. In fact, there is no strict distinction between these two terms. The major difference is the origin. Pervasive computing is more industry driven, whereas ubiquitous computing originally stemmed from academia and it had a more visionary connotation. In this book, we do not differentiate either but prefer the term "pervasive" as it—solely from the semantics of the term—suggests that related technologies *pervade* our daily lives and stay unobtrusive and invisible. The semantic of "ubiquitous" rather suggests that computational entities may be everywhere and omnipresent, which is clearly not what human beings aspire for and which leads to the impression of being counterproductive.

Pervasive computing is roughly the opposite of virtual reality [181]. Where virtual reality puts people inside a computer-generated world, pervasive computing integrates computers into the peoples' real world. Virtual reality is primarily a problem of performance and resources. Pervasive computing, in contrast, faces difficult challenges in bringing together human factors, computer science, engineering, and social sciences. The Elsevier Journal of Pervasive and Mobile Computing[3] states that the "goal of pervasive computing is to create ambient intelligence where network devices embedded in the environment provide unobtrusive connectivity and services all the time, thus improving human experience and quality of life without explicit awareness of the underlying communications and computing technologies. In this environment, the world around us (e.g., key chains, coffee mugs, computers, appliances, cars, homes, offices, cities, and the human body) is interconnected as pervasive network of intelligent devices that cooperatively and autonomously collect, process and transport information, in order to adapt to the associated context and activity."

The resulting pervasive environments are characterised [14, 113, 146] by high dynamics, steady changes in network topologies, low bandwidth, frequent disconnections, resource-restricted devices, and less user-friendly interaction possibilities (e.g., smaller screens, no keyboard or mouse etc.). Thus, the major challenge lies now in appropriate engineering of pervasive environments such that a match of the physical world with the abstract world of virtual resources succeeds in order to provide an unobtrusive added-value to users [146]. Kindberg in his article [99] refers to this as "physical integration" and derives from this the *Boundary Principle* which states that pervasive system designers should divide this combined world into "environments with boundaries that demarcate their content. A clear system boundary criterion—often, but not necessarily, related to a boundary in the physical world—should exist. A boundary should specify an environment's scope but does not necessarily constrain interoperation." Human life takes place in discrete environments, which should be considered in the engineering of pervasive environments. The world, thus, consists of several pervasive systems instead of *the* pervasive system. This is closer to reality and also seems to be easier in realisation as system boundaries are narrower and less variables and constraints need to be considered. Important, however, is the guaranteed interoperability with other pervasive systems. Consequently, another characteristic pervasive systems must respect and integrate is spontaneous interoperation [99]. As components and entities in pervasive environments are subject to steady change and dynamics they must be capable of spontaneously interoperating. From this, Kindberg derived the *Volatility Principle* [99] stating that pervasive systems should be designed on "the assumption that the set of participating users, hardware, and software is highly dynamic and unpredictable. Clear invariants that govern the entire system's execution should exist." System designers should consider system-wide invariants that facilitate addressing volatility.

Kindberg [99] identified several challenging areas within the field of pervasive computing that must be investigated in order to develop useful and successful future services. One of these is programming paradigms for middleware layers. Various such paradigms are deployable for pervasive systems. One example is the *message-oriented* middleware. The main idea is that software processes communicate by sending messages. The advantage of such systems compared to low-level concepts (like plain sockets or remote procedure calls) is that the communicating entities do not have to be available at the same time. This allows for asynchronous communication. The middleware layer deals with the appropriate delivery of the messages and stores the messages in queues. This is basically done in two ways: either in a one-to-one pattern (point-to-point), where an addressable queue associated to each entity exists, or in a one-to-many pattern (i.e., publish-subscribe). One entity can subscribe to a certain topic and consequently is allowed to receive all messages that are put into the

---

[3]See http://www.elsevier.com/wps/find/journaldescription.cws_home/704220/description

queue representing this topic.

In a *service-oriented* middleware, all the functionalities are encapsulated in service providing entities which are distributed over the participating entities. These services are well-known and the interfaces are defined in a standardised way by using a type of a description language. Each interaction of service providers and service consumers is independent of each and every other interaction. To support dynamics, most systems incorporate some form of a registry (i.e. "yellow pages") where service providers announce their service and the details on how to find and use them. Service consumers, in turn, only have to know this registry to search for and deploy services. In order to support heterogeneity, most service-oriented middleware systems are abstracted from the underlying hardware and operating system, thus, allowing platform independence.

A *Web-based* middleware is similar to a service-oriented middleware, concerning the way it describes and makes use of services. However, it is based on and deploys existing, ubiquitous and well-established infrastructure or standards like HTTP and XML and is thus targeting Web technologies. The most common and prospering implementation of a Web-based middleware is Web Services. The Web Service technology uses the Simple Object Access Protocol (SOAP) as the communication protocol, which, in turn, is independent of the protocol for actual information exchange[4], the Web Service Description Language (WSDL) for describing the services and the Universal Description, Discovery and Integration registry (UDDI) as a central yellow page facility for listing the services.

A *component-based* middleware is comprised of various components encapsulating different tasks and functionalities. A component is a reusable program building block which can be either tightly or loosely coupled with other, possibly distributed, components to perform a certain task. It has a clearly defined interface and conforms to a prescribed behaviour common to all components within an architecture. Components can furthermore be nested and/or be composed to form another component.

An *agent-based* middleware subsumes a network of distributed and largely autonomous computing entities (agents). An agent is defined as "an encapsulated computer system that is situated in some environment, and that is capable of flexible, autonomous action in that environment in order to meet its design objectives." [185] An agent represents a problem solving entity focused on a specific task. It possesses social abilities, like it is able to communicate with other agents in a high-level way at the knowledge layer, and thus is able to co-operate, negotiate and coordinate [92]. It has control over its internal state and behaviour, that is it has autonomy. It is intelligent to a certain extent and it has knowledge of itself and the world and is able to reason and decide. An agent can behave reactively (i.e., it responds to simple stimuli in a straightforward manner) or proactively (i.e., it has the ability to reason about his objectives and to try to do everything necessary to reach these goals). It interacts with the embedding environment through sensors and actuators, where this environment or agency provides all the necessary functionalities for the agents to exist and to accomplish their tasks. Agents are much more likely to adapt to change, which is inherent to pervasive environments.

According to Kindberg [99] and several further authors [46, 63, 111, 112, 138, e.g.] another middleware paradigm that is very appropriate for pervasive environments are *tuple space* systems. The characteristics of pervasive environments—where disconnections have to be regarded as the rule rather than the exception— favour a decoupled and opportunistic style of communication. With decoupled we mean that computation needs to proceed even if entities are disconnected. Opportunistic refers to the fact that connectivity has to be exploited whenever it becomes available. The synchronous communication paradigm supported by many traditional distributed systems has to be replaced by a new asynchronous communication style. [112] The first

---

[4]This could be HTTP or SMTP, for instance.

tuple space system is Linda and was introduced by David Gelernter and Nicholas Carriero in 1985[5] [69]. The idea behind this paradigm is to have a (distributed) shared object space where processes can have access to. Shared objects (i.e., tuples) can be put into the space, removed from the space or just read, which implies that they remain there. To demonstrate, a process A could place a tuple containing any information into the space without knowing any other processes. Another process B could remove or read that tuple at any time without knowing A. The communication act would be complete. A does not have to care if its tuple is read and when, by whom it is accessed and who eventually removes it from the space. The two processes can run on different types of machines, different hardware and different operating systems. They do not have to run at the same time, process A for instance can be terminated long before process B actually gets alive [64]. This paradigm inherently addresses the Volatility Principle and offers a high degree of temporal, spatial, and referential decoupling.

Adaptation is another key research area in pervasive computing as identified by Kindberg. It involves several sub-areas which are necessary to conduct adaptations at all. Examples are location detection, or activity sensing and recognition. Hence, context-awareness—where context naturally is much broader than only location and activity[6]—is of prime interest. Providing services according to context, in fact, *is* the unique selling proposition of pervasive environments [151,152,154]. One of the first definitions of context was elaborated in [150,151] stating that it comprises computing, user and physical properties. Later in 2000, this definition was extended by adding time as a further aspect [39]. The widest-accepted definition of context in the pervasive computing community is the one introduced in [56], which states that context is any information which can be used to characterize the situation of an entity, where an entity is a person, place or object that is considered relevant to the interaction between a user and an application, including the user and the application themselves. Hence, there is a broad variety of possible context parameter. In [1], the authors propose that for pervasive environments it shall be classified according to primary and secondary context types, where the primary ones (location, identity, activity, and time) cause the greater effect and should be considered for characterising situations.

Other research areas related to pervasive environments engineering cover topics like hardware (miniaturisation of devices, increase in performance and functionality, like sensor boards), networking (mobile ad-hoc networks or sensor networks), security and privacy, usability and human-computer interaction (HCI) (such as novel interfaces), and self-organization of devices and services. We do not address these areas in this book in detail as it is not the prime focus of the presented research work.

To conclude, in pervasive environments information and services relevant for users are dependent on more different context factors and also the period of validity is shorter due to frequent context changes of involved entities (such as location). Network connections offer less capabilities and disconnections are rather the rule than the exception. The user interaction possibilities are more restricted, too, such as smaller devices, smaller screens, restricted or no keyboard, no mouse, or power dependency on batteries. Thus, entities and technologies involved in pervasive environments are more heterogeneous and the evolving configurations more complex compared to stationary ones. From this fact, we deduce that in such environments the demands on *coordination* are higher, which has also been observed earlier in [61].

Due to the diversity inherent to pervasive environments and their particular characteristics, *coordination* is a further major issue [61]. The coordination entities usually are highly constrained stemming from the particular characteristics as outlined above. Systems for applications in pervasive environments, for instance, need to be able to process the dependence on different types of context—such as acting entity, activity, location, and time.

---

[5]In fact, the very first idea of this concept was introduced in 1982 and was called "Global Buffer" [71]. Linda was introduced in 1985.

[6]The Free On-line Dictionary of Computing defines context as "that which surrounds, and gives meaning to something else" (http://foldoc.org).

In this work, the focus is on coordination and is explicitly investigated in the scope of mobile collaboration, i.e. mobile users collaborating in pervasive environments. One example of an application area of mobile collaboration is emergency management, which is introduced in the following Section 3.1.2.

3.1.2 Emergency Management

Emergency management (EM) is an application area that inherently deals with mobile collaboration. The research conducted in this book is applied, tested and evaluated to representative collaboration scenarios out of this domain. For this, some basics about EM need to be understood. This Section introduces relevant concepts of emergency management.

An emergency is a broad term which includes rapid natural and man-made hazards containing avalanches and railway accidents, drought, famine or disease and disaster events that have a different time lapse like floods or forest fires. Emergencies have severe consequences. Emergency management subsumes the activities of emergency operators necessary to prevent and relief such situations [41].

Typically, already medium-sized emergencies involve several organizations each one subsuming many operators that are finally present and need to be coordinated. It is, however, essential to understand that such organizations are strictly organized in hierarchies. Hence, the smallest "collection" of operators that is combined to one logical unit is a team (often simply called a "group") which never subsumes more than ten human beings. Clearly, several groups are combined to the next level logical unit, which is mostly referred to as a "platoon[7]". Platoons again are combined to further more high-level classifications. Thus, to increase efficiency operators are divided into units, where the smallest unit in EM is the group with a size usually not larger than ten members working collectively on one task. Close collaboration happens mainly within groups; thus, representing a mobile, collaborative work environment and an appropriate area of application for the coordination architecture.

Emergency management processes comprise several phases. A typical EM cycle (see also Figure 3.2) includes the following phases [76]:

1. *Risk assessment and planning:* This phase involves strategic planning and locating potential emergency management problems. With the help of an ICT-based EM system such hazards can be identified more easily, the consequences evaluated, and thus, recovery plans established.

2. *Mitigation:* Based on the outcomes of the analysis, appropriate actions shall be accomplished such as reinforcing constructions or relocation of potentially endangered infrastructure. Monitoring means can be set up at critical locations. The goal is to prevent or reduce the harmful effects of an event.

3. *Preparedness:* This includes activities for preparing emergency responses and workers such as contingency planning, model building, and training.

4. *Response:* The critical activities immediately following an incident are conducted in this phase. Emergency workers have to stabilise the situation and to speed up the recovery process, too. ICT and collaboration technology can aid here in understanding the scope, complexity, and severity of the incident. Consequently, appropriate actions can be defined more rapidly and accurately such as directing personnel to specific locations equipped with required tools, organizing medical support, establishing evacuation routes, monitoring the current situation to avoid any secondary damage, providing logistical support, and ascertaining unavailable services and infrastructure.

---
[7]This structuring according to logical units is common in any organisation around the world. Merely, there are differences in naming.

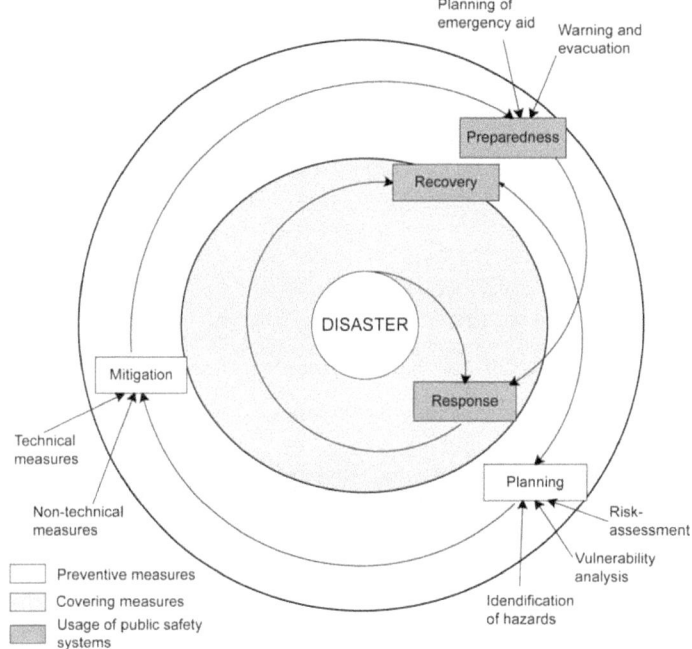

Figure 3.2: Disaster Cycle [104]

5. *Recovery:* Recovery efforts start when the threatening emergency situation is over. These efforts are usually separated into two phases; *(i)* Short-term: The main task is identifying the damage on site and generating priority plans. Critical decision makers monitor the recovery process and can request the current status by consolidating information; also from remote locations. *(ii)* Long-term: This implies restoring all services to normal state, which may take several years. Activities involve, for instance, replacing infrastructure and homes. ICT can again be deployed for prioritising and documentation and finally, for determining costs.

Each of the above phases is inter-related and can be supported and even improved by ICT-based CSCW [12, 54].

Emergency situations are, by nature, very heterogeneous. In [54], these are divided into three basic categories[8]:

1. *Knowledge of activities – knowledge of time and place*

---
[8]Potentially, a fourth type in this classification would be *no knowledge of activities – knowledge of time and place*, which is not relevant because as soon as time and place are known the activities can be defined and planned

This category is not very critical, especially because the structures are well known, relatively static, well proven, and there is enough time for preparation of the emergency management activities (e.g. in advance announced events such as festivals, concerts or demonstrations).

2. *Knowledge of activities – no knowledge of time and place*
   This case involves highly trained and specialised teams that are able to respond to particular incidents, which are by nature very similar. The teams adhere to well proven practices, train appropriate skills, and can plan their activities well in advance without exactly knowing the concrete occurrence (e.g. car accident or local fire).

3. *No knowledge of activities – no knowledge of time and place*
   Such situations are characterised by sudden occurrence, unpredictability, diversity, and usually magnitude (e.g. earthquakes, floods or men-made hazards like explosions or acts of war or terrorism).

The third type represents the most challenging facet and is the prime subject of our research because it comprises the highest degree of uncertainty and unpredictability. Due to its severity and dimension, a configuration of diverse organizations (such as police, paramedics, military, private organizations, etc.) is involved in order to deal with the situation, where (ICT-based) mobile collaboration technology can be availed.

Communication is essential for the coordination of different tasks [174] reducing the complexity of interaction between and among the teams with respect to inter- and intra-organizational information exchange. Because of inherent unpredictability of such emergency situations, it is impossible to define the communication channels nor to place the needed equipment at the site prior to the event. Instead, teams and configurations of teams have to be formed quickly, and the communication infrastructure has to be established spontaneously; ideally, without requiring any extra environmental means such as communication facilities or electricity, which might not be available in such emergency situations. Moreover, the emergency site can be spatially distributed connecting the involved nodes and leading to a spreading of the responses and distribution of public safety teams. Coordinative efforts are very high and without proper collaboration of the involved organizations an effective emergency relief becomes more difficult [115]. Thus, a collaborative behaviour is inevitable.

The persons in charge do usually not possess the complete knowledge about the current situation and the position and activities of the responses; they lack the global view. Additionally, the human factor must not be neglected, such as the complexity of social structures and social roles, communication habits, individual preferences, and feelings like anger, fear, stress, uncertainty, or panic. Providing support through technology is not trivial as such situations usually are critical. In certain scenarios, however, and up to a certain extent technology, indeed, can assist emergency operators [51].

An important pre-condition for an application that is finally accepted by the user is to obey the major claim of pervasive computing (as argued in Section 3.1.1), namely to have the technology stay in the background and assist human users in an unobtrusive manner.

In this book we want to present a system that shall help to gain benefits from exploiting coordination theory by applying it to collaboration in pervasive environments, which represents a showcase to exemplify the optimisation potential that lies in addressing coordination. The following Section 3.2 discusses the design and engineering process of such a system.

3.2 CorA – A Coordination Architecture for Pervasive Environments

In this Section we want to propose a system that shall alleviate exploiting the optimisation potential in the field of mobile collaboration. This system is a coordination architecture that can be deployed by pervasive information system developers. We present the system design and implementation. The engineering of our coordination architecture (CorA) is based on requirements stemming from analyses of pervasive computing scenarios.

3.2.1 The CorA System Design

This Section covers the scenario-based requirements analysis, the design of the coordination architecture, the communication infrastructure (which is a tuple space based approach with according replication strategies) and coordination patterns.

3.2.1.1 Requirements Analysis

In order to design a coordination architecture to address the broad spectrum of current and future collaboration systems for pervasive environments, we found it fundamental to examine several well-known examples of relevant scenarios. The term "scenario" is somehow overloaded and may mean several things. The notion of scenario in the fields of human-computer interaction (HCI), object-oriented software engineering, and requirements engineering (RE) ranges from real world descriptions and stories in a rather informal and narrative style (also with the use of pictures) to formal models and specifications (structured models, tables, UML diagrams etc) [164]. Also the scope may range from a very general, abstract, broad, and high-level description to very concrete facets of real world situations such as a single example of an event sequence [4]. In a more technical context, a scenario may also represent a use case, a specific path through a use case of a software system or other event sequence descriptions of system components [165].

Scenarios can be exploited for a great range of different usages, such as requirements analysis, user–designer communication, for example to motivate design rationale, envisioning (to help imagine a future system), software design, implementation, training, and documentation [35].

In this book we use diverse well-established and accepted scenarios as a vehicle to derive essential requirements that shall be met by pervasive information systems. A thorough requirements engineering process in its strict sense is out of scope of this book and would require close collaborations with a set of users for whom a specific computer system is intended. The goal of this work is to devise a coordination architecture on a much broader basis. Consequently, the derived requirements are not as specific as the ones resulting from RE methodologies such as SCRAM[9] or CREWS[10] but are rather on a coarse basis. Nevertheless, they depict a general direction where future information systems shall be heading to and which functionality these need to provide. This scenario-based approach was essential for us to start reasoning about how to design CorA to meet current and future needs.

From the scenario-based analysis, we derived relevant commonalities which were eminent in each of these scenarios, and took these as the basis for the derivation of requirements. These requirements express characteristics that must be addressed by any proposal aiming at effectively and successfully providing well-coordinated

---
[9] Scenario-based Requirements Analysis Method (SCRAM) [164].
[10] Cooperative Requirements Engineering With Scenarios (CREWS) [80].

ID	Source	Scenario	Main Characteristics
1	ISTAG	Maria - Road Warrior	Personalisation, mobility
2	ISTAG	Dimitros and D-ME	Privacy, seamless connectivity
3	ISTAG	Carmen: traffic, sustainability [...]	Seamless interaction
4	ISTAG	Annette and Solomon in the Ambient [...]	Mobile collaboration
5	Amigo	Home Information & Entertainment	Personalisation, unobtrusiveness
6	Amigo	Home Care & Safety	Automatisation, personalisation
7	Amigo	Extended Home Environment	Adaptive remote interaction
8	DAIDALOS	Automotive Mobility	Seamless inter-device communication
9	DAIDALOS	Mobile University	Seamless service invocation, interaction
10	WORKPAD	Disaster Relief	Mobile collaboration
11	CASCADAS	Living Diary	Seamless service invocation, pervasive content sharing
12	CASCADAS	Blog Cafe	Pervasive advertisement, service provision

Table 3.2: Overview of Investigated Scenarios

services in pervasive environments.

As sources for our examinations we took the Ambient Intelligence (AmI) scenarios of the IST Advisory Group (ISTAG)[11] and the EU projects Amigo[12], DAIDALOS[13], WORKPAD[14], and CASCADAS[15]. The detailed description of these scenarios is available on the Web (as indicated by the footnotes). Table 3.2 summarizes these scenarios.

To discuss the requirements derived from the analysis of the scenarios investigated, for each of the requirements we summarize the requirement in general terms (as derived from the analysis of different scenarios) and relate to it an identifier Rx, where x is a consecutive number. Table 3.3 shortly summarizes the above identified requirements.

R1: Enrichment of the physical world with (virtual) data sources
A user while being on the move might be interested in a certain object of the physical world and wishes to get further information delivered. From that we derive: *Technical representations of pervasive environments must be able to enrich information coming from the physical world by merging it with information from other (virtual) data sources. (R1)*

R2: Context-sensitive queries for integrated data sources
Various occurring data sources may be represented by different kinds of physical or virtual sensors, exhibiting different formats, quality, or quantity. Only a generalizing intermediary data model can help to harmonize and provide an interface for context-sensitive queries. We derive that: *Pervasive environment representations must provide an expressive data model that allows to appropriately integrate various data sources and context-sensitive queries. (R2)*

R3: Context-dependent data refinement
Pervasive services require personalized information. In order to provide this information relevant to specific situations of a user, a model allowing context-sensitivity is necessary which at the same time has to be open and extensible in the sense of being able to contain data from most diverse sources. This means that: *Pervasive environment representations must allow for a refinement of data according to the specific context of the user's*

---
[11] http://cordis.europa.eu/ist/istag.htm, Document: ftp://ftp.cordis.lu/pub/ist/docs/istagscenarios2010.pdf
[12] http://www.hitech-projects.com/euprojects/amigo, Document: Deliverable D1.2
[13] http://www.ist-daidalos.org, Document: Deliverable D111
[14] http://www.workpad-project.eu, Document: Deliverable D1.3
[15] http://www.cascadas-project.org, Document: Deliverable D5.1

current situation. (R3)

R4: Increased flexibility through decoupled and opportunistic communication

The dynamics of pervasive and mobile environments are particularly challenging from the reliability viewpoint. On the one hand, communications are subject to frequent changes and prone to steady disconnections. On the other hand, the data itself is of a highly dynamic nature, and one cannot guarantee neither access to specific data nor reliability and stability of data. Thus, to provide the necessary flexibility it is essential to avoid both tightly-coupled communications and tightly-coupled access to data. This results to: *Pervasive environment representations must address flexibility and dynamics through decoupled communication and information distribution. (R4)*

R5: Ability to handle network disconnections

If uplinks to centrally maintained services are not available due to a disconnection, some sort of redundancy of services and information must be envisaged. If a network access is not possible, at least the locally available devices should be able to interact, respectively, devices and selected services must be able to function in a stand-alone mode. Hence, we derive that: *Pervasive environment representations must provide a minimum set of services/information even when the network connection is not ideal. (R5)*

R6: Ability to address diversity to tackle complexity

Due to technological advances, hardware is getting more powerful and smaller at the same time. Various hardware entities already exist and the number and diversity is increasing. Pervasive information systems have to take this into account. This means that: *Pervasive environment representations must be prepared to address the increased complexity resulting from the multitude and diversity of involved entities and technologies. (R6)*

R7: Explicit integration of coordination mechanisms

In the examined scenarios, coordination is either explicitly or implicitly steadily reoccurring. Environments must be accordingly engineered to integrate appropriate concepts to facilitate coordination. We conclude that: *Pervasive environment representations must address the increasing need for coordination of coordinables by appropriate mechanisms as it is a precondition for the delivery of the required service quality. (R7)*

R8: Reusable coordination solutions

A considerable number of problems related to coordination activities are common to all scenarios and exhibit a high degree of similarity. Thus: *Pervasive environment representations must provide standards and generally applicable models for (re-)use for reoccurring problems. (R8)*

The following Section discusses how we exploited these findings and how this influenced the architectural design of CorA.

3.2.1.2 The Layered Coordination Architecture

To address the potential complexity of pervasive environment representations (as from requirement $R6$), as a result of our investigation on the requirements (Section 3.2.1.1), we conceive the necessity of a separation of concerns. As a consequence, we decided to abstract several functionalities—derived from the captured

ID	Requirement
R1	Pervasive environment representations must be able to enrich information coming from the physical world by merging it with information from other (virtual) data sources.
R2	Pervasive environment representations must provide an expressive data model that allows to appropriately integrate various data sources and context-sensitive queries.
R3	Pervasive environment representations must allow for a refinement of data according to the specific context of the user's current situation.
R4	Pervasive environment representations must address dynamics and flexibility through decoupled and opportunistic communication and information distribution.
R5	Pervasive environment representations must provide a minimum set of services/information even when the network connection is not ideal.
R6	Pervasive environment representations must be prepared to address the increased complexity resulting from the multitude and diversity of involved entities and technologies.
R7	Pervasive environment representations must address the increasing need for coordination of coordinables by appropriate mechanisms as it is a precondition for the delivery of the required service quality.
R8	Pervasive environment representations must provide standards and generally applicable models for (re-)use for reoccurring problems.

Table 3.3: Listing of Derived Requirements

requirements—into functional entities, which are interdependent. Thus, the coordination architecture CorA is organized as a layered architecture where each of the six defined layers encapsulates specific functionalities (see also Figure 3.5). The *factual data* layer offers the means for capturing and keeping data from the physical and virtual world (*R1*). To combine both worlds and to have means to beneficially integrate data coming from diverse sources the *data model* layer exploits a context model (W5) (*R2*). Furthermore, as this model is designed to address context information according to several dimension (actor, activity, space, and time, which are the prime context factors [1]), we try to satisfy *R3*. Due to the decoupled and opportunistic way of communication, tuple spaces best address the Volatility Principle (introduced in Section 3.1.1) and hence *R4*. We adopt a tuple space-based approach (see also Section 3.2.1.3) for the *tuple management*, which is capable of covering the provision and up-to-dateness of the data integrated in the context model. As the tuple management layer is responsible for acting locally on a device, the *tuple distribution* layer provides added-value by interconnecting different entities. This layer is responsible for establishing a network and hence, a federated tuple space that is constituted by the available nodes (*R5*). *R6* is addressed by the openness of the adopted context model and the tuple-space approach which can account for arbitrary types of information.

As CorA reflects a coordination architecture for pervasive environments and *R7* is the "coordination requirement", several layers are responsible for addressing this requirement. To provide improved coordination various aspects are necessary and for this a combination of several CorA layers is needed: data model, tuple management and distribution layer. The *coordination* layer accomplishes the coordinative activities of the potentially great magnitude of occurring entities (*R6*) according to defined laws (*R7*). Reoccurring coordination problems are subsumed in pattern-based solutions (*R8*) on this layer. The *application* layer, finally, represents the interface to the user and provides the requested services or application, respectively (*R6*, *R7*). Table 3.4 summarizes these decisions based on requirements.

A further insight conceived during the examinations was that due to the overwhelming amount of heterogeneous pieces of information coming from various sources, and pervasive services, which shall be accessible in an anytime, anywhere, and anyhow manner, future pervasive information systems are inescapably going to be more complex. We derived that such systems will require sophisticated coordination strategies (see requirements

Design Decision	Requirement(s)	Comment	Page
Layered architecture	R6	Appropriate method to show the dependencies of various concepts and to decompose different concerns	–
Factual data layer	R1	Provides the factual data sets coming from the physical and the virtual world	28
Data model layer	R2, R3, R7	Proposes the W5 concept as the data schema for context-sensitive queries according to four dimensions	28
Tuple management layer	R4, R7	Integrates the usage of tuple spaces	30, 32
Tuple distribution layer	R4, R7	Covers appropriate information management (e.g., replication strategies)	31, 35
Coordination layer	R6, R7, R8	Encapsulates the resolution of interdependencies through laws within the business logic or patterns	31, 39
Application layer	R6, R7	Subsumes pervasive entities, agents and/or services	32

Table 3.4: Overview of Design Decisions Related to Requirements

R6, R7, and R8) in order to appropriately address the rising magnitude of user requirements, constraints, and interrelations and hence, the need for context-sensitivity.

Moreover, it has been observed—during the scenario-based analysis and in literature—that several types of coordinative behaviours are highly similar, often reoccurring, and typical for specific situations [55, 58]. Consequently, various coordination laws and mechanisms can be subsumed to so called patterns (see the coordination layer of CorA, Section 3.2.1.2), which shall provide standardized means to assist in these situations. A detailed discussion of various coordination patterns is provided in Section 3.2.1.5 or in [19].

Collaboration applications usually span three dimensions: *(i)* number of people, *(ii)* degree of goal completion, and *(iii)* degree of decoupling [12]. The coordination architecture CorA as intended in this work addresses a rather low number of collaborating people (i.e., below 15). The target application area emergency management usually involves several teams. Every team as the smallest unit, however, comprises about ten team members which is subject to the collaboration in CorA. The degree of goal completion denotes the degree how close people work together to reach a common goal. Emergency management is a very collaborative application area implying many goals that must be reached collectively. Hence, emergency management—as all other critical application areas with real-time constraints and danger of life—represents one of the areas with the highest degree of joint goal completion. Finally, decoupling refers to the distribution in time and space (see also Table 3.1 on page 13). Emergency management operators are naturally spread over the whole emergency site and means for asynchronous communication are indispensable. This orientation of CorA along the three dimensions is illustrated also in Figure 3.3.

As a first architecture break-down, the necessary high-level building blocks of the coordination architecture were identified to be the following components [18]: communication, coordination, data model, and collaboration application. Figure 3.4 depicts this as a block diagram influenced by Klein's 3C model [100] (see also Figure 3.1 on page 12). This is a first de-composition and design step in order to build CorA.

Based on this first break-down and on the requirements analysis presented in Section 3.2.1.1 above, we continued with developing a more fine-grained model. Figure 3.5 depicts the layered coordination architecture of CorA. The interfaces between the layers are defined by API calls indicated by the boxes labelled "API IF" between each layer (for details we refer to the implementation Section 3.3). The business logic sub-part of the coordination layer is always strongly connected to a respective application on the top most layer. Hence, it must be implemented together with that application and no interface can be provided by CorA. The rounded rectangles in Figure 3.5 of the tuple management and tuple distribution layer depict the fact that these layers contain several elements such as the tuple management layer may be capable of holding and managing several local tuple spaces. The following Sections describe each layer in more detail and relate them back to the defined requirements.

Number
of People
CorA
Degree of
De-coupling
Degree of Goal
Completion

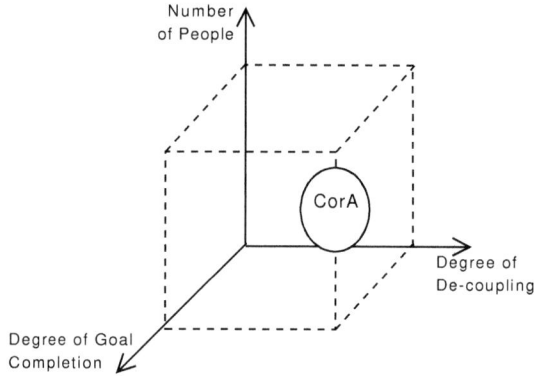

Figure 3.3: Positioning CorA

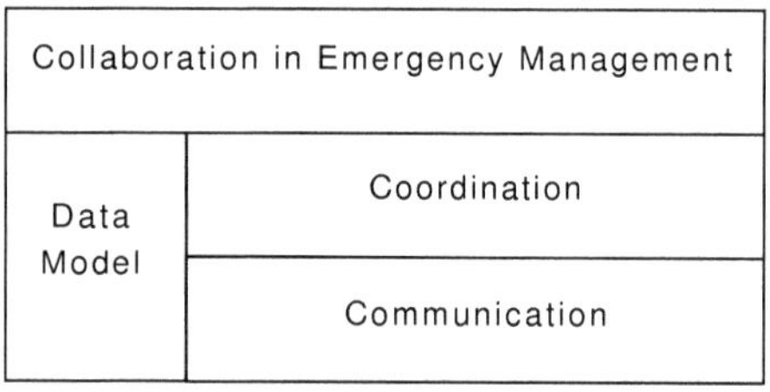

Collaboration in Emergency Management
Data
Model
Coordination
Communication

Figure 3.4: Conceptual Overview over Main Components

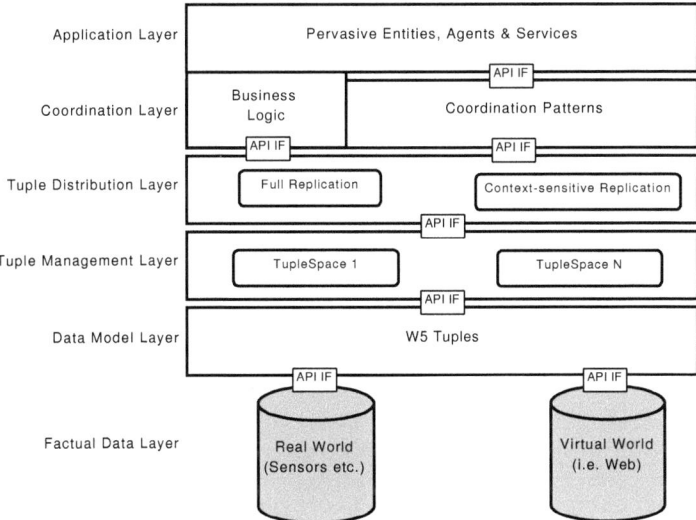

Figure 3.5: Overview of the Layered Coordination Architecture (CorA)

Factual Data Layer

In order to provide the necessary support in pervasive environments—particularly for collaborative applications—the possibility of navigating physically integrated information spaces that can represent a detailed model of the world has to be considered [99]. Present as well as historic data about its entities, its processes, and its social structure need to be considered. For this, a proper merging and integration of information coming from two distinct sources must be supported: *(i)* from the *real world* (i.e., through pervasive devices or things such as sensors), which due to their proximity to the (mobile) user can be directly accessed and any environmental characteristic of the physical world can be acquired and information generated or processes triggered; or *(ii)* from the *virtual world* (i.e., the Internet or the Web), which shall enable the actors (agents, users etc.) to dynamically and on-demand retrieve additional information related to their current situation (i.e., context-sensitivity). We denote these either physical or virtual data as "facts". Also, the actors within the environment can be described by facts. Consequently, facts can also represent information about actors (e.g., software agents) such as their state or activities, which is a necessary prerequisite for our coordination environment to enable either direct or indirect coordination between entities in a decoupled way.

To build a comprehensive data model that allows for integrating various sources, the separation into facts coming from real and virtual world sources is necessary. By this, real world information can be enriched on-demand with information from virtual sources (*R1*).

Data Model Layer: The W5 Model

The great magnitude and heterogeneity of potentially resulting amount of facts require for an expressive, yet simple model to represent this information about the two worlds of the factual data layer. Such a data model must provide means to *model* and *combine* information coming from heterogeneous sources, enable ease of querying and processing, and should account for adaptation to context and incomplete information. Our proposed context model considers that diverse data about facts can be expressed by means of a five-fields tuple (*Who*, *What*, *Where*, *When*, *Whatabout*): "someone or something (*Who*) does/did some activity (*What*) in a certain place (*Where*) at a specific time (*When*)" This was originally specified in [36] where the authors introduced the W4 context model with simple and extensible semantics. Within the work of this book, however, we recognised the need for a fifth field in the tuple: *Whatabout* which describes necessary meta-information about that tuple that serves for self description and can also be exploited for distribution and replication (see Section 3.3.2 for a comprehensive listing). We refer to this extension as the W5 model.

Subsequently, each field is described in more detail. The examples used in the following passages are oversimplified and mentioned for clarification. Each field contains an optional *type* classifier and the mandatory *value*. The used notation is: `type:value` or `value` if no classifier is given or necessary. The representation of the five fields in the concrete implementation of CorA is complex and introduced in the corresponding Section 3.3.2.

The *Who* field associates a subject to a fact and represents an actor. *Who* may represent a human being, an unanimated part of the context acting as a data source (e.g., the ID of a sensor or an RFID tag), or the name of a Web resource. The *Who* field also contains information about the type of an entity. Examples for valid entries for this field are: `firefighter:Smith` or `tag:tag#567`.

The *What* field describes the activity performed by the subject. This information can either come directly from the data source (e.g., a sensor is reading a temperature value) or be inferred from other context parameters (e.g., an accelerometer on a PDA can reveal that the user is running), or it can be explicitly supplied (e.g., content of a Web page). The information contained in this field is at least a description of the type of the activity and information about the activity itself. For example, valid entries for the *What* field are: `reading:"Principia Mathematica"`, `meeting:control_room`, or `read_temperature:23`.

The *Where* field associates a location to the fact and thus represents a spatial description. In the model, the location may be a physical point represented by its geographic coordinates (e.g., longitude, latitude), a geographic region, or it can also be a logical place. Web resources, for instance, are also expressed as logical places by using a URI. In addition, context-dependent or relative spatial expressions like `here` or `radius:300m` can be used for context-aware querying.

The *When* field associates a time, a time range or time periods to a fact and is referred to as a temporal description. Valid examples are `2006/10/17,1753`, `range:1600-1715` or `periode:6h`. Also in the case of the *When* field, context-dependent expressions can be defined (e.g., `now`, `yesterday`, `later:2h`) and used for context-sensitive querying.

Pragmatical considerations led us to the decision to introduce a new field holding meta-information about tuples: the *Whatabout* field. It contains information such as a universally unique identifier (UUID), a timestamp when the tuple was created, in which type of potentially different repositories (i.e., tuple spaces) it is stored, whether changes should be kept in a history, or if it is intended to be kept only locally on the device. Moreover, this field contains information about the tuple's "age" (in form of the version vector concept which is introduced later in Section 3.2.1.4) and the type of replication protocol relevant for this tuple.

The W5 concept relies on the assumption that software agents can be associated with data sources (i.e., providers of facts) and can create W5 tuples and insert them into shared repositories or data spaces. These spaces are referred to as tuple spaces (see tuple management layer on page 30). Data are sensed from different available sources by diverse sensors such as RFID tags, location (GPS receivers), motion, temperature, or software sensors collecting information from virtual sources. Information then is inferred by combining them in a W5 tuple. Due to the nature of pervasive environments (see also *R4*), these sensed data may change frequently. W5 tuples can be generated continuously and thus can account for keeping dynamically changing data up-to-date. The *When* field and relevant meta-information in the *Whatabout* field are responsible for processing and providing this timely information. By interpreting these fields, querying entities can deduce the timeliness of a W5 tuple. Moreover, a history of generated tuples can be constructed and kept in the tuple spaces.

Some examples should clarify the concepts of the W5 model: Firefighter Smith is present on an emergency site and currently moving quickly. An agent running on his GPS-enabled portable device periodically (e.g., every 10 seconds) creates a tuple corresponding to his activity and position. The position is stored according to the GPS National Marine Electronics Association (NMEA) format. This example is illustrated in Figure 3.6[16].

Moreover, the model is not restricted to human beings but in an abstract sense every coordinable entity can represent an actor. Consequently, also states or activities of any entity can be modelled in W5. A W5 tuple of a software agent controlling a SunSPOT[17] sensor (*Who*) may be composed as depicted in Figure 3.7. This

---

[16] For readability the *Whatabout* field is omitted in Figures 3.6 and 3.7 as it is not necessary for the basic understanding of the concept.
[17] See `http://www.sunspotworld.com/`

```
Who:   firefighter:Smith
What:  running:7kmh
Where:nmea:$GPRMC,191419,A,4505.4690,N,01350.7140,E,
            0.0,0.0,170807,0.4,E,A*19
When:  periode:10s
```

Figure 3.6: W5 Tuple Example 1

```
Who:   sun-spot:www.sunspotworld.com/semacode-spot0815
What:  sensing_light:0815
Where:emergency_site
When:  ts:1173085856
```

Figure 3.7: W5 Tuple Example 2

sensor determined the brightness (*What*) at the defined emergency site (*Where*) on Monday, March 5, 2007 at 09:10:56 (*When*). This timestamp (ts:1173085856) is encoded as the Unix epoch time representation, which is the time in milliseconds elapsed since January 1, 1970 00:00:00 UTC.

According to coordination theory, a description of four (abstract) entities is necessary to resolve interdependencies: actors, activities, constraints, and interdependencies itself. By using W5, we provide a means to accordingly model these entities: *Who* reflects the actors, *What* the activities, and the constraints can be defined by *Where* and *When*. The interdependencies cannot be directly modelled by W5 but are addressed in the higher coordination layer (see Section 3.2.1.2).

The W5 concept can be exploited for context-sensitive coordination along four different dimensions of context (actor, activity, space, and time), which—as they are accordingly represented in the data model—can, in turn, be availed and combined as needed to address the specific context of an actor in a particular situation. By adopting W5 tuples, we provide a way to semantically combine diverse data from different sources (*R2*) into one data model, which then can be exploited to provide additional and context-dependent information to the user (*R3*). It provides a unique and well-defined interface for upper layers of CorA to access heterogeneous facts (*R7*).

Tuple Management Layer

Due to the inherent properties of decentralized (i.e., peer-to-peer-based) architectures—such as scalability and fault resilience [3]—and their appropriateness for mobile environments [97], the tuple management layer of CorA is entirely based on unstructured peer-to-peer (P2P) concepts. We refer to Appendix 5: Definition 10 or [21] for a definition of P2P networks. Concretely, we deploy a decentralized tuple space-based computing approach [133,138], which is very similar to Linda-like systems [69]. As opposed to the idea of this original Linda system, which assumed one existing central and persistent data space, this approach is completely decentralized. Every involved node carries a local space and may be replicated with the other available participants of the mobile ad-hoc network (MANET) according to variable strategies, which are covered by a higher layer (tuple distribution layer).

Querying agents or entities can retrieve knowledge facts via simple pattern-matching query mechanisms; i.e., through associative addressing of information stored in tuples which through the underlying W5 model allows for context-dependent queries even when the information is incomplete. The local tuple space may be separated into several logical sub-spaces each containing different types of information (i.e., tuples). A general challenge for this infrastructure is to identify strategies for evaluating which tuple space separations are necessary, which tuple to store in which space, and which tuples need to be distributed to other peers in the network and when. Such decisions may depend on many factors, such as access control, performance, or scalability reasons.

Due to the inherent decoupling mechanisms of space-based approaches (see Section 3.2.1.3), the tuple management layer ideally addresses $R4$, i.e. flexibility, which is a prerequisite for delivering services in appropriate quality ($R7$).

Tuple Distribution Layer

In order to appropriately and reliably distribute information—which in CorA is stored in form of W5 tuples—a space overlay was developed where peers residing on each of the involved participants are responsible for the distribution of the tuples among the tuple spaces according to appropriate replication strategies. Basically, two diverse types of tuple distribution respectively replication have been designed: *(i)* full, or *(ii)* context-sensitive replication. The former strategy is adopted for necessary and indispensable—and ideally "lightweight"—information (such as addresses) because it might face scalability problems soon.

The second strategy allows for tuple replication based on the four context dimensions covered in the W5 data model (i.e., actor, activity, space, and time) and also a combination of these. Consequently, tuples can be distributed more effectively, resulting in less data transmission overhead, less costs, and increased performance. Moreover, information can be provided to the requesting entity in a context-sensitive way through exploiting the five fields of the W5 data model. Hence, the delivered information can be much better targeted to the exact needs of the information requester.

The tuple distribution layer extends the functionalities of the underlying tuple management layer and adds the connection between the local spaces to constitute a federated "quasi-global" space. Hence, this layer is related to covering the same requirements as the tuple management layer, namely $R4$ and $R7$.

The Tuple Management and Distribution Layers are essential parts of the approach of this research work. Therefore the separate Sections 3.2.1.3 and 3.2.1.4 are specifically devoted to these layers.

Coordination Layer

The coordination layer provides mechanisms to be used for the resolution of the most important element of coordination theory: the *interdependencies* (as introduced in Section 2.2). These are usually implicitly addressed by encapsulating the coordination laws within the business logic of an application. We propose, however, a separation of programming from coordination concerns [13] and by this provide ways of explicitly addressing the resolution of interdependencies. General coordination problems shall be addressed by deploying coordination patterns. This generalization is a cognitive process—not restricted to information system design and implementation or Computer Science at all—where people naturally look for similarities in the world to derive patterns. Subsequently, these can be deployed as best-practices for problems of the same or similar type. As a consequence, the problem solving process can be alleviated and accelerated by using a well-known method.

To deploy a pattern, the coordination problem has to be understood first. Second, the potential solution to the problem can be looked up in a coordination pattern catalogue and the most suitable solution can be chosen. Every pattern comprises different entities, describes the interdependencies and how to resolve them. Patterns denote the least common denominator such that it can be deployed generally. To address specific requirements, it has to be adapted accordingly. The patterns have to be supplied with the necessary input and, subsequently, according to its internal coordination laws, they generate output: a solution to the coordination problem.

The patterns concept in CorA can be deployed in two ways: *(i)* Available reference implementations of coordination patterns in the form of programming libraries can be adopted by invoking the relevant APIs such as the supervisor/worker pattern introduced in [20]. *(ii)* Specifications of patterns as in [19] can be accordingly implemented, which is very similar to the way design patterns are exploited in software engineering [67]. Examples of coordination patterns would be location-oriented coordination, meeting, or negotiating.

If, however, one problem cannot be resolved by patterns because it is too specific or unique it is addressed by implementing the appropriate laws within the business logic, which as a negative effect, may lead to poor extensibility, interchangeability, or re-usability.

Standardized solutions—such as patterns—alleviate problem solving processes through re-usability. Hence, the coordination layer covers $R8$. Furthermore, pattern-based coordination is directly linked to optimizing coordination and consequently the service quality ($R7$). The issues raised in $R6$, in turn, are highly depending on coordination and coordination patterns.

This layer covers an essential part of the book. Therefore, the separate Section 3.2.1.5 is devoted to this layer.

Application Layer
The application layer describes the interfaces to calling entities which are necessary to provide pervasive services or applications. Atop applications or application-level services can make use of the underlying CorA layers and encapsulated functionalities as required in an anywhere and anytime fashion.

The application layer comprises the heterogeneous, pervasive entities (e.g., mobile equipment), mobile users, or their surrogate (software agents) ($=R6$); respectively denote the interface to these. Finally, this layer shall provide the requested services in an according quality as claimed in $R7$.

In the next Sections we deal with selected and relevant topics of CorA in more detail.

3.2.1.3 Tuple Spaces in Pervasive Environments

As argued in Section 3.1.1, Linda-based [34, 69] systems are very appropriate as middleware paradigm for developing pervasive information systems. A great degree of flexibility due to inherent decoupling mechanisms can be reached. These decoupling mechanisms are threefold: *(i) spatial* decoupling: two processes can reside in completely different computational environments and communicate via the space, *(ii) temporal* decoupling: the processes do not have to be available at the same time in order to communicate (i.e. asynchronous communication), and *(iii) referential* decoupling: entities can communicate with each other and request data without addressing each other directly. There is no need to "know" each other.

With respect to the data distribution, also in CorA a tuple space-based approach is adopted (i.e., tuples as the atomic representation of data). The main difference, however, of the classic Linda system compared to the tuple spaces in CorA is that we implement a *decentralization* and *distribution* of several spaces throughout the network of participating peers. The initial Linda system was a server-based architecture representing a bottleneck and hampering flexibility. Only later implementations of Linda considered multiple spaces (such as in [70] or [87]). The tuple space implementation within CorA, however, complies with P2P considerations. Due to its small footprint, it is possible to deploy the tuple space kernel on mobile and portable devices. These features make it a light-weighted middleware suitable for mobile ad-hoc networks. Every involved peer interacts directly with its own local tuple space. Through rich replication mechanisms (see subsequent Section 3.2.1.4) on CorA's tuple distribution layer, the local tuple spaces are merged to a "global federation" of all tuples spaces of available peers at the time.

The following paragraphs describe the main concepts and operations of Linda-like tuple spaces. It should be mentioned that these concepts and operations are—in an abstract sense—very similar or the same in all tuple space-based architectures[18]; which is also true in the case of CorA. Merely, the designation of method names differs.

Besides the tuple space, which represents the virtually shared memory or repository, the concept of a tuple (i.e., a data structure, Definition: Appendix 5: 12) kept within the repository is central to any tuple space-based architecture. Each tuple is a finite collection of typed data fields—or objects in terms of the object-oriented paradigm—and is an atomic unit as fields cannot be taken and altered independently. The whole tuple has to be processed at once. A tuple τ_1 can be composed as follows:

$$\tau_1 = (``\text{Hello World}'', 3.1415, \text{false})$$

Because τ_1 contains an ordered sequence of three typed values (the string "Hello World", the double 3.1415, and the boolean false), its arity is three and its type signature is (**string, double, boolean**). All fields are so called *actuals* as they all represent actual values. Tuple spaces also offer the possibility to have formal values, i.e., *formals*. Another tuple τ_2 may be composed of actuals and formals:

$$\tau_2 = (\text{i:integer}, ``\text{A string}'', \text{b:boolean}, 4711)$$

τ_2 now has the arity four and the type signature is (**integer, string, boolean, integer**) where the first and the third fields are formals.

Tuples do not have an explicit address and, hence, can only be addressed and retrieved by their contents (i.e., content-addressable data structures [69]). This adds additional flexibility as addresses or IDs need not to be known. Tuples are identified via associative matching by using the arity and type signature information. Formals can be used as "wild-cards".

Linda—as the classic representative of a tuple space—offers the following operations to interact with the space: With the unblocking **out(τ)** operation a tuple τ is inserted to the tuple space. The blocking

---
[18]For a discussion on other tuple space systems refer to the Related Work Section 4.4

and destructive in(τ) operation takes the first tuple matching τ which is a template, returns it and deletes it from the space, where τ can consist either of formals, actuals, or both. If no tuple matches, the process that issued the in() operation is suspended until a matching tuple is available. If multiple tuples match, the one returned is selected non-deterministically. The blocking and non-destructive read(τ) operation is similar to in() but does not delete the tuple from the space. The following example illustrates these concepts.

```
Process #1
1 τ₁ := (''Linda'', 1.5, true)
2 out(τ₁)
...
3 τ₂ := (''CorA'', 1, true)
4 out(τ₂)


Process #2
1 τ_Template := (s:string, i:integer, b:boolean)
2 in(τ_Template)
```

Assume that processes #1 and #2 are running concurrently. Process #1 inserts τ_1 by issuing out(τ_1). At the same time, process #2 creates the template tuple $\tau_{Template}$ and asks the tuple space to take a corresponding tuple from the space (by in($\tau_{Template}$)). As no matching tuple has been inserted yet, process #2 is suspended. Note that τ_1's type signature is (string, double, boolean) and hence is not matching the type signature of $\tau_{Template}$ (string, integer, boolean) but τ_2 is. As soon as process #1 inserts τ_2, process #2 is notified and τ_2 is immediately retrieved by this process and deleted from the space.

Reasonable extensions to the presented operations are non-blocking in() and read() operations and operations—so called bulk operations [145]—that allow the insertion of several tuples and the retrieval of not only one but all matching tuples. We refer to these operations as out_all(), in_all(), and read_all(). The classical Linda model suffered from a problem known as the "multiple read" problem [145]. If a process wishes to perform a read on *several* tuples then in the classic model all the tuples must be destructively retrieved, processed and then returned to the tuple space. This requires a lot of processing effort and is error prone especially if other processes are adding and removing tuples during this ongoing operation.

The semantics of original Linda are non-deterministically and, hence, do not specify which tuple is returned if there is more than one tuple that matches a template. It is not specified that a different tuple is returned if another read is performed on an unchanged tuple space. Indeed, the usual implementation is to return the first matching tuple, if the tuple space does not change then the same tuple will be returned each time. The introduced bulk operations are a way to solve this problem.

Such extensions have already been implemented by either later versions of Linda or other tuple space-based architectures and are also deployed in CorA. Section 3.3.4 discusses the concrete APIs that CorA provides to interact with the tuple space.

3.2.1.4 Replication Mechanisms in CorA

Replication in distributed systems is the process of keeping more than one image of a data item (i.e., *replica*) on several nodes or peers. Resources are kept redundant in order to improve accessibility and scalability— thus, performance—and fault-tolerance—thus, reliability. In distributed systems—like CorA—several aspects of transparency need to be addressed in order to deliver the required behaviour [166]. One of these is replication transparency[19]; i.e., a user or service requesting access to a data item can do so without noticing that this item may exist several times in the network. Concurrency and consistency issues are completely masked.

The most intricate challenge of replication lies in keeping the distributed copies of data items mutually consistent. Due to the nature of distributed systems—nodes are connected by network technologies—it cannot be guaranteed that all replicas of one data item are identical at all times. Rather replication management has to provide mechanisms for all replicas of the same item to converge after an update into a mutually consistent state [12]. An action triggered by a user or service performs an operation on the logical data item. The underlying middleware maps this action to operations on the multiple copies available in the network. To be correct, this mapping must ensure to perform a sequence of actions on replicated data equivalent to a correct execution of actions on non-replicated data. This requirement is called the *one-copy serialisability* criterion [89]. Methods that shall satisfy this criterion are referred to as *replica control algorithms*. One-copy serialisability requires that different replicas are mutually consistent. In general, there are two types of failures that need to be addressed by replica control algorithms: *(i)* node/peer failures and *(ii)* communication failures. The former describes the case when one or more peers keeping replicas in the network become inaccessible, due to any reason such as a hardware crash. The latter is more disruptive and denotes a disconnection between one or more peers leading to network partitions. The remaining peers are partitioned into groups. Peers in each group can communicate among each other but cannot communicate with peers from other groups. Replica control algorithms need to guarantee mutual consistency after a rejoin of groups as soon as recovered from the communication failure. The one-copy serialisability criterion needs to be satisfied.

Two basic types of replica control algorithms are available: *(i)* optimistic *(ii)*, or pessimistic [47]. If a failure occurs, optimistic algorithms do not place any restrictions on processing data in any partition. It is assumed that changes on replicas in different partitions do not conflict, or arisen conflicts can be resolved, respectively. Pessimistic algorithms, however, prevent inconsistencies from occurring by limiting access to data a priori. Each partition makes a worst-case assumption about what might happen in other partitions and processes the data under these assumptions. To achieve this, pessimistic algorithms naturally entail a larger communication and processing overhead than optimistic algorithms. A comprehensive introduction to pessimistic replica control algorithms such as primary site, active replication (state machine, atomic broadcasts), and voting (majority consensus, weighted voting, hierarchical voting, dynamic voting) can be found in [12] and will not be elaborated further in this work as it is out of scope. In CorA, an optimistic replica control algorithms is adopted.

Due to the characteristics of pervasive environments, pessimistic replica control algorithms are too static and too resource intensive. Some form of *lazy* replication is much more appropriate [75].Hence, in CorA we developed an algorithm based on *version vectors* [134] which is an optimistic algorithm. The particular setting of CorA does not allow us to differentiate between peer failures or communication failures, which is another reason why we have chosen version vectors this method does not require a distinction. Each replicated data item

---
[19]Others are access, location, migration, concurrency, failure, persistence.

which in CorA is a tuple is associated with a version vector V. In the original proposal by Parker et al., the size n of that vector corresponds to the number of replicas (i.e., the number of copies of tuples stored by peers) of that tuple. Whenever a tuple τ is changed this is reflected in the version vector and the other (reachable) tuples and their corresponding vectors are updated. In its simplest form, at peer j the ith vector entry v_i counts the number of changes in τ originating from peer i. Additional information can be tracked too and appears to be reasonable in most cases. Thus, in CorA this algorithm is changed such that we do not only count the updates but store the time (in form of a time stamp) when the update happens. By counting the time stamp entries per replica we can infer the number of updates processed on each tuple.

A vector V of a replica is said to *dominate* another vector V' of a replica of the same tuple, if the following expression holds true:

$$\forall i \in \{1, ..., n\} : v_i \geq v'_i$$

If the vector V dominates V' then in V more updates arrived. Thus, V' represents a subset of V and can easily be adapted. Two vectors are said to *conflict* if they are different and neither dominates. This is the case when the replicas have received different updates. Then the replication logic has to deal with it where such cases can become quite complex. CorA has to deal with such cases, too. The example depicted in Figure 3.8 illustrates the procedure as proposed by [134]: A network consists the three peers {P_1, P_2, P_3} each holding one replica of a tuple, which is denoted by the initial version vector associated with that tuple: < P_1:null, P_2:null, P_3:null >. No updates have been conducted yet. Let us assume that a partition happens due to any reason into two groups: {P_1, P_2} and {P_3}. Now, two updates happen in the first group (indicated by two plus signs in Figure 3.8 underneath the corresponding peer P_1). Then, peer P_2 leaves the one group and joins peer P_3. At this time two updates happen concurrently: one in the first group (again by peer P_1) and one in the second group (by peer P_3). Finally, both groups rejoin resulting in a conflict of the two version vectors:

< P_1:{TS_{11},TS_{12},TS_{13}}, P_2:null, P_3:null >
and
< P_1:{TS_{11},TS_{12}}, P_2:null, P_3:{TS_{31}} >

This conflict needs to be resolved by appropriate replication and consistency logics within CorA where each of the different fields of the tuple needs to be examined and updated accordingly. The authors are aware that it might well happen that some inconsistencies cannot be resolved such as two concurrent updates of exactly the same field data. In that case, errors may occur and the pragmatic approach to solve this problem is—to the best of the knowledge of the authors—taking the most recent change on the tuple τ_i. The other, older datum is, nevertheless, kept in a separate tuple τ_{i-1} which is stored in the same tuple space and related to τ_i as a "historic" tuple.

Section 3.3.2 gives more details about how the version vector algorithm is concretely implemented in CorA.

The version vector algorithm can also deal with the fact that we cannot assume that the initial partition, i.e., the known set of connected peers during start-up, is complete. As over time other peers, which may all be mobile, may dynamically join and leave the current partition the version vector simply grows or shrinks

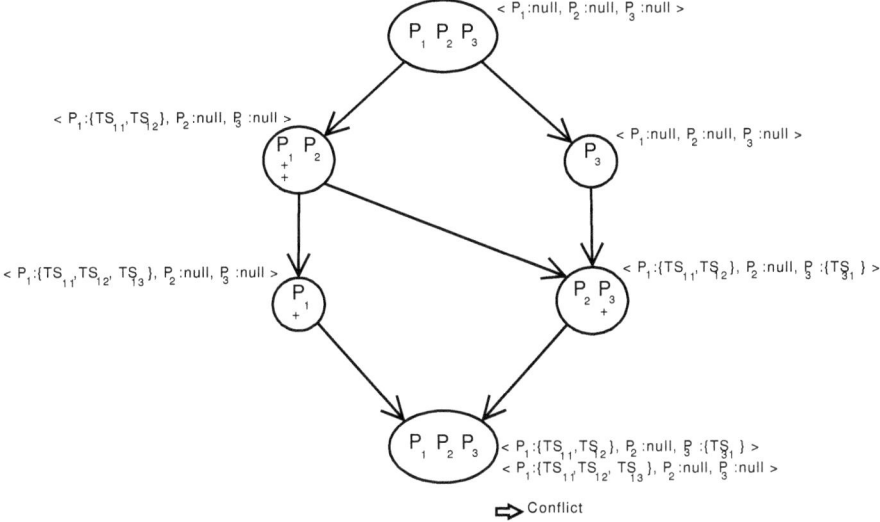

Figure 3.8: A Version Vector Example

accordingly. The algorithm does not differentiate and treats these cases equally, which again makes it very appropriate for deployment of replication in pervasive environments.

Moreover, under normal conditions[20], a minimum of connectivity is always provided as an application or service can connect to and access the local tuple space, thus, embodying an abstract network with two peers. This is guaranteed as every peer in a CorA network has its own local space and replication mechanisms start operating as soon as connectivity between remote peers is available. This fact already causes a relaxation of the error-proneness and sensitivity for inconsistency of the CorA middleware for data distribution in a pervasive information system.

Building up on the concept of version vectors, different replication strategies are deployed in CorA. Basically, it can be differentiated between two base strategies: *(i)* full replication, and *(ii)* context-dependent replication. The former is "expensive" in terms of using network resources and the potential danger of inconsistencies regarding the contents of the distributed local tuple spaces. Some information, however, needs to be fully and permanently replicated such as address information (i.e., how to address the other peers in the network). The latter is much more resource-sensitive, more sophisticated but also more complex to design and implement.

Both strategies exhibit two further policies: *push (event-based)* and *pull (on-demand)*; and can exchange one or more tuples in each replication transaction. This construct can be best described along two dimensions as

---

[20] Referring to the fact that as soon as an application using CorA is started also the local tuple space is mandatorily instantiated and available.

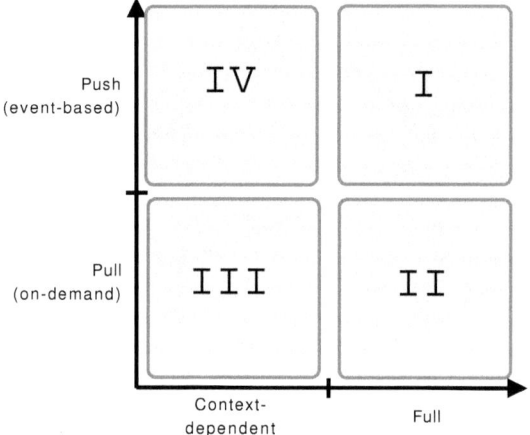

Figure 3.9: Overview of the Replication Strategies

depicted in Figure 3.9), in which the y-axis denotes the two policies, and the x-axis the strategies. The further it is progressed on both axes, the more traffic is produced. There is a direct correlation.

The four replication mechanisms are described as follows:

1. **Full Replication – Push** (Square I). One or more produced tuples are sent from one peer to all currently connected peers. If not already existent in the remote peers the tuple(s) is/are stored there. Otherwise all fields are updated according to the new values. This strategy usually is the reaction to an event.

2. **Full Replication – Pull** (Square II). Peers can explicitly and on demand ask other peers for one or more tuples which are then transferred to the querying peers.

3. **Context-dependent Replication – Pull** (Square III). Peers can dependent on the described context request certain fields of tuples. The described context does not necessarily have to be their current context but can be any context which is necessary. The context is described by the fields of the W5 model, hence in principle to four dimensions (actor, activity, space, and time) plus meta-information.

4. **Context-dependent Replication – Push** (Square IV). Peers can also subscribe to events and get required fields of tuples event-based and in a context-dependent way. The subscribers define the event, the particular context, and the information (contained in fields) they are interested in. The peers that can provide such information and listen to the requested events deliver this information as pushed tuples as soon as an event during the defined context happens.

These four strategies are elaborated and formally described in Section 3.2.2.2. The concrete implementation can be found in Section 3.3.

3.2.1.5 Coordination Patterns

When working on something, building something or encountering problems, people naturally do not tackle this by steadily inventing new solutions but recall similar activities or problems which had already been solved. As this was successful once, the essence is applied again. This expert behaviour—i.e., thinking in problem-solution pairs—is roughly what is described as a *pattern* [27]. Patterns can help to exploit the collective experience of experts. Every pattern embodies a well-proven solution to a specific, recurring problem. This concept is domain-independent and has been explicitly reported in architecture [2], economics [59], social interaction [58, 126], and computer science; in particular in software engineering [9, 27, 43, 44, 67], middleware design [64, 86, 170], agent technologies [5, 55, 98], and workflow and business process management [175]. By abstracting from specific problem-solution pairs and extracting common factors generic patterns can be generated.

This current use of the term pattern is deduced from the writings of the architect Christopher Alexander who wrote several books on urban planning and building architecture. He presumably has a greater impact on computer science than on architecture[21] [27]. Many of his thoughts and concepts are applied to object-oriented programming as software design patterns. In his book "The Timeless Way of Building" [2, p. 247] he writes about patterns (in architecture):

> Each pattern is a three-part rule, which expresses a relation between a certain context, a problem, and a solution.
>
> As an element in the world, each pattern is a relationship between a certain context, a certain system of forces which occurs repeatedly in that context, and a certain spatial configuration which allows these forces to resolve themselves.
>
> As an element of language, a pattern is an instruction, which shows how this spatial configuration can be used, over and over again, to resolve the given system of forces, wherever the context makes it relevant.

Hence, each pattern as a minimum is described by three cornerstones: *context*, *problem*, and *solution*. The context describes a situation that gives rise to a problem. This problem, in turn, is recurring in that particular context. The solution represents a proven resolution of that problem in the context. A pattern defines a type of rule that establishes the relationship between these as it is a solution to a problem in a particular context [27]. All three cornerstones are closely coupled. Moreover, according to Buschmann et al. patterns share several properties (adapted from [27]):

- A pattern addresses a recurring design problem that arises in specific design situations and presents a solution to it.

- Patterns document existing, well-proven solution design experience. (Patterns are not created artificially but evolved out of the experience of practitioners. Their knowledge has been made explicit and accessible for others, too.)

- Patterns identify and specify abstractions. (Typically a pattern describes several abstracted components involved and necessary to solve a problem and details their responsibilities and interdependencies.)

---

[21] Christopher Alexander was invited to give the keynote at the 1996 Object Oriented Programming Conference OOPSLA which turned out to be a seminal speech with respect to patterns applied to computer science.

- Patterns provide a common vocabulary and understanding for a common problem. (By choosing appropriate pattern names and terms these can evolve to a common vocabulary which facilitates discussions without the need for extensive explanations.)
- Patterns support re-usability and extensibility. (When a specific pattern is applied others—familiar with patterns—can easily reuse the deployed components and correctly extend them if required because they perfectly understand the pattern, its goal, and its internal logic.)
- Patterns help in devising and managing complex and heterogeneous systems. (Patterns can act as building-blocks as parts of larger systems. They can serve as a "toolbox" for component-oriented system design. Moreover, by decomposing a system by using patterns, it can be conceived and managed easier and faster.)

Animated by these properties of patterns, the intention in CorA, too, was to establish a pattern catalog that shall address common coordination problems and provide applicable solutions. In addition, the above quote of Alexander shows the close relationship between coordination and patterns. In all the different domains mentioned above where patterns are relevant those patterns are essentially used to *coordinate* something by using a well-known and proven schema. A certain parallelism to coordination theory and the five entities of coordination as introduced in Section 2.2 is observable: *Actors* performing *activities* are obviously involved otherwise a problem would not exist. The *actors* exploit a pattern to support their *activities*. The required problem solution is the *goal* the *actors* (collectively) want to achieve. The context, system of forces, and the respective configuration—as mentioned in the quote—can be matched to the *constraints*. The pattern itself encapsulates and proposes the rules and mechanisms to resolve the interdependencies present in the relationship between the actors, the context, the problem, and the forces. Hence, applying a pattern is already some form of "standardised" coordination. However, in the Coordination Layer of CorA we propose to support coordinative endeavors by explicit coordination patterns because also with regard to coordination, it has been observed that certain coordination problems are reoccurring and show many similarities [55].

Taking the above considerations into account, for the purposes of CorA we define

> A coordination pattern is a three-part rule that proposes a generic solution to a coordination problem as a relation between a certain context, a certain system of forces that occurs repeatedly in that context, and a certain configuration of coodinables, interdependencies and coordination laws that allow these forces to resolve themselves[22].

A *pattern language* is now used to describe such a pattern, the necessary details, and the way how the solution can eventually be reached. Coplien defines a pattern language as "a structured collection of patterns that build on each other to transform needs and constraints into an architecture" [44, p. 312] (See also Appendix 5: Definition 15).

In the following passages we provide a catalogue of reusable coordination patterns using a pattern language. In formulating the introduced patterns [19, 20] we particularly catered to the characteristics of pervasive environments discussed in Section 3.1.1. The patterns can be applied to the relevant coordination problems (i.e., context) in pervasive environments. The pattern language subsumes the following properties: name, context, problem, solution, implementation, known use, and related patterns.

---

[22]See also Appendix 5: Definition 14

The Supervisor/Worker Pattern

In pervasive environments, in particular in collaboration scenarios of mobile users, one fundamental and omnipresent facets of coordination is the relationship between one responsible entity that distributes tasks to other entities that have to work on these and finally deliver the results. The corresponding coordination activities are encapsulated in the *supervisor/worker* pattern.

Context
In order to increase fault-tolerance, efficiency, exchangeability and hence, scalability the possibility of concurrent execution in pervasive, distributed systems shall be exploited. For this, identified tasks and subtasks shall be distributed and executed by various worker-entities simultaneously and the results shall be collected and presented to the supervisor-entity.

Problem
In a collaborative scenario in a pervasive environment, how can a certain goal that involves the completion of several—possibly interdependent—tasks be reached more efficiently and effectively?

Solution
The supervisor is responsible for achieving the overall goal by specifying subtasks and distributing those among the involved entities embodying the workers. Respectively, subtasks may have to be dynamically redistributed according to changing environments. Finally, the supervisor collects and reassembles the outcomes of the subtasks and stores or reports the solution. The workers execute the assigned tasks and reply the outcomes. The availability of worker peers may be characterised by frequent joining and leaving behaviour which shall be addressed by the supervisor through according strategies.

Implementation
Figure 3.10[23] depicts a UML class diagram of the supervisor/worker coordination pattern. The `Supervisor` and `Worker` classes are both inherited from the `Actor` entity. Each `Actor` is associated with a `Constraint` and in particular with a `Capability` class, which is mostly relevant for the workers as they are characterised by their capabilities. Supervisors create `Task` objects and workers after being assigned by a supervisor process `Task` objects. Tasks are further sub-classed by `SubTask` and `Result`. In addition each task can aggregate an arbitrary number of `TaskDependencies`.

Known Use
A typical application of of this pattern would be in parallel computation [69] or in distributed systems [27] where several computing entities with specific capabilities are available. Emergency management represents an adequate application example [115].

Related Patterns
In [27], the master-slave pattern is described which addresses similar scenarios. However, differences are that slaves are usually created by the master and are represented by equal entities offering the same service executing equal subtasks. In contrast, workers of the supervisor/worker pattern are heterogeneous entities offering specific capabilities. Moreover, the supervisor inheres some form of control functionality

---
[23] The UML class diagrams used in this whole Section 3.2.1.5 are simplified ones in order to increase readability. For instance, getter and setter methods are omitted. Also the access specifiers are not depicted. Generally all attributes, however, are **private** and the methods of the pattern-related classes are default, i.e., **package**.

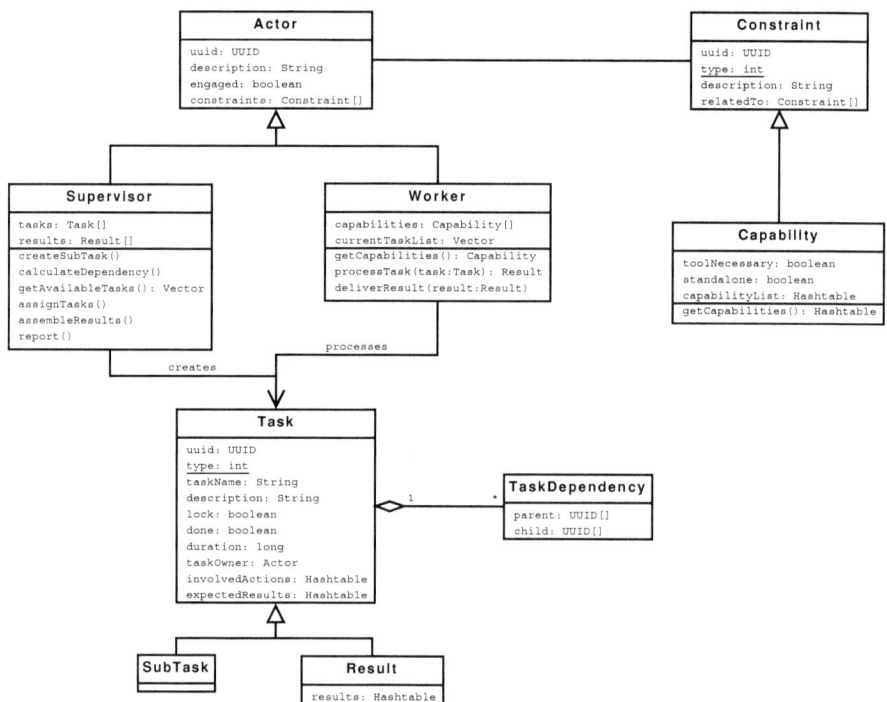

Figure 3.10: Class Diagram of the Supervisor/Worker Coordination Pattern

which monitors and guarantees the proper execution of the subtasks in the correct sequence, and the final assembly, which is not addressed in the master-slave pattern. Consequently, the supervisor entity requires appropriate protection means as it represents a potential target for malicious intentions.

The Location-oriented Coordination Pattern

People unaware of a location naturally orientate themselves by the help of particular and distinct objects [161]. We use particular points in time and space in order to coordinate our activities. Such so called "focal points" (or also Schelling Points) were described by Game Theorist Thomas Schelling in [149]. During several experiments, Schelling discovered that people in order to approach mutually beneficial results tend to use very characteristic spots in time and space, which also works without direct communication. For instance, Schelling asked people where they would meet a stranger in New York while the stranger also wants to meet them but they cannot communicate. A substantial majority answered: "under the clock in Grand Central Station at noon".

As this specific concept of (location-oriented) coordination is a natural human behaviour, it is intuitive and broadly accepted. It was our motivation to improve coordination in pervasive environments by adopting this concept and implementing it within a computational system. By interacting with this system, mobile users shall be supported in their activities by the embedded algorithms which provide the mechanisms to resolve the interdependencies related to location-oriented coordination.

We exploit this concept for developing a coordination pattern that shall support people in decision-making and coordination of activities in pervasive environments (such as in collaborative applications). We call this pattern *location-oriented coordination* (LOC).

Context
Responsible entities or authorities need to reason or decide upon certain facts. In many cases–particularly in pervasive environments–available resources are volatile and frequently changing. As a result, information is incomplete or only an excerpt of the whole information present, which may lead to low-quality or wrong decisions. In the context of coordination, most of general decision-making processes imply reasoning about spatial information and are often based on distinctive spatial objects (Schelling Points) [149] or on map-based representation of spatial information. We refer to this mode of coordination as the Location-oriented Coordination (LOC) pattern.

Problem
The lack of "global" knowledge of mobile users may lead to wrong or suboptimal decisions or outcomes, respectively. Coordination of activities cannot be conducted effectively. How can actors be provided with distinct information about temporal and spatial objects (being consolidated to a "quasi global" knowledge) which can be exploited to base decision on.

Solution
To assist people in their decision-making processes, a (visual) representation of the current position of relevant objects or people is provided. This implies that distinctive spatial objects are used to improve the coordinative activities in dynamic, pervasive environments.

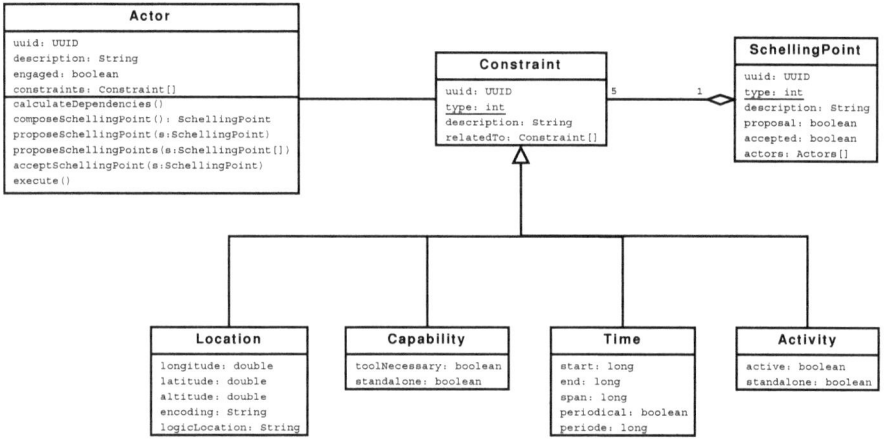

Figure 3.11: Class Diagram of the Location-oriented Coordination Pattern

Implementation

Figure 3.11 depicts a UML class diagram of the location-oriented coordination pattern. The **SchellingPoint** class aggregates several **Constraints**. These are sub-classed by specific types of constraints such as **Location**, **Capability**, **Time**, or **Activity** and can be extended on demand. The main coordination logic is encapsulated in the **Actor** class that calculates dependencies out of the constraints, composes, proposes, and finally accepts Schelling Points.

Known Use

Intuitively, people steadily use spatial objects, for instance, to determine a meeting point, i.e. using spatial information to coordinate their activities. The concept of wayfinding through landmarks [161], for instance, is a novel approach to navigation systems.

Related Patterns

No concrete related pattern is known. A similar approach is coordination via environmental cues [131], where entities are coordinated by the possibility of reading present cues in the environment or "tagging" spatial objects with certain cues for others.

It it important to mention that this location-oriented coordination pattern is independent from any implementation. In general, patterns can be deployed either by using the programming libraries of available reference implementations of patterns, or by implementing specifications similar to the way design patterns are exploited in software engineering [67]. In *our* coordination architecture all the classes are realised as W5 tuples and kept within the distributed tuples spaces. Communication (e.g., between the **Actors** when the **proposeSchellingPoint()** method is invoked) is exclusively conducted by W5 tuple exchanges via the tuple spaces.

Meeting Pattern

A meeting is a very natural way of coordination. Human beings regularly meet for the sake of coordination or simply for communication or keeping one other up to date. This type of coordination is described and exploited in the meeting pattern.

Context
Due to the great diversity of involved stationary and mobile, loosely coupled entities in pervasive environments, it is not trivial to appropriately coordinate their activities. Direct messaging is often not possible–due to spatial dislocation–or even not desired as it would lead to tight coupling and consequently to inflexibility. Hence, a commonly-known meeting point shall either be introduced a priori or shall be determinable in an ad hoc manner. Actors may use meeting points for coordination.

Problem
How can decoupled and heterogeneous entities (such as actors) coordinate their tasks and mediate or synchronize their activities in pervasive environments?

Solution
A dedicated named meeting point–in time and space–has to be either predefined which is statically located somewhere in the environment. Or the actors must possess the necessary knowledge to agree upon a well-known meeting point during runtime. This point and its characteristics such as its address, which may change over time, have to be announced to all relevant participants of the distributed system. Hence, processes know how to address and access this meeting point at certain times. Furthermore, it is possible to call for meetings, announce one's interests, register, or being notified about changes.

Implementation
Figure 3.12 depicts a UML class diagram of the meeting pattern. The meeting pattern exploits the extensibility and re-usability properties of patterns. It uses the location-oriented coordination pattern for retrieving Schelling Points as illustrated in Figure 3.12. Schelling Points ideally represent a potential meeting point for actors. The `Actor` class queries the LOC pattern package for potential Schelling Points and represents them as `MeetingPoint` objects. All the logic for organizing, proposing, planning, and performing meetings is encapsulated in the methods of the `Actor`. In addition, this class aggregates an arbitrary number of `ScheduledActivity` objects denoting the activities scheduled for a meeting. These, in turn, aggregate `Action` objects which are the concrete actions to be executed.

Known Use
Several software agent-based systems deploy this approach.

Related Patterns
This pattern is based on the observer pattern [67], which additionally provides the functionality of monitoring and coordinating the activities necessary for the operation of a meeting place.

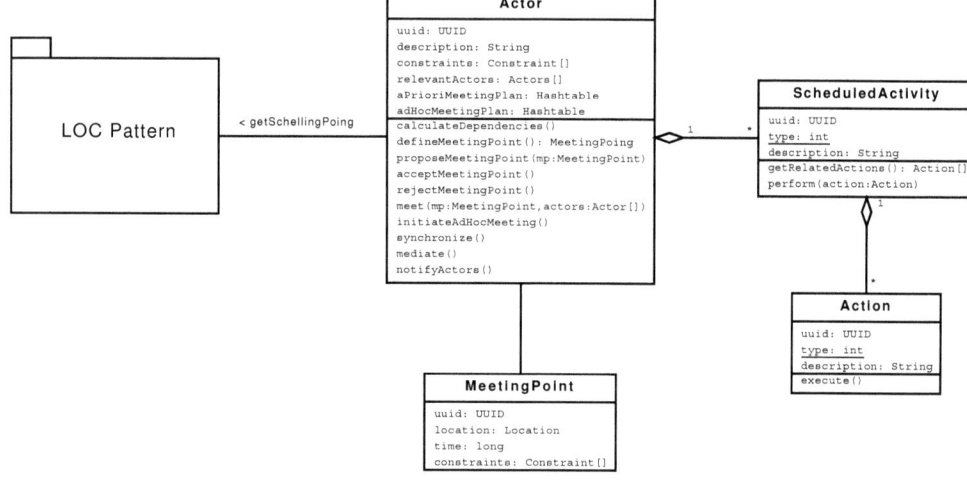

Figure 3.12: Class Diagram of the Meeting Pattern

Blackboard Pattern

A blackboard can be exploited as a common and well-known platform for information exchange and postings. It is useful if entities cannot communicate directly with each other. Instead they can communicate indirectly by help of a blackboard.

Context

In case of equal actors with the same rights and privileges which are co-operating on certain tasks, a medium shall be in place which assists in their coordination and synchronisation process, allows for information exchange and deposition and hence, facilitates mutual progress.

Problem

How can coordination of equal, distributed and highly decoupled entities be realised—also in cases where concrete addresses are not explicitly known?

Solution

An additional intermediary entity has to be introduced which can be used to store information and thus, can be used to distribute or retrieve information. For instance, a virtual blackboard can be used to store intermediate results which serve as input for other dependent activities of a certain task. With this mechanism, actors do not have to explicitly address others but move the relevant data onto the blackboard from where it can be retrieved or modified by according receivers. A publish/subscribe mode [10][24] of

---

[24] Although publish/subscribe messaging paradigm was first described in [10] the credit should go to Frank Schmuck, who probably was the first person to invent a fully functional publish-subscribe solution in his PhD project [155].

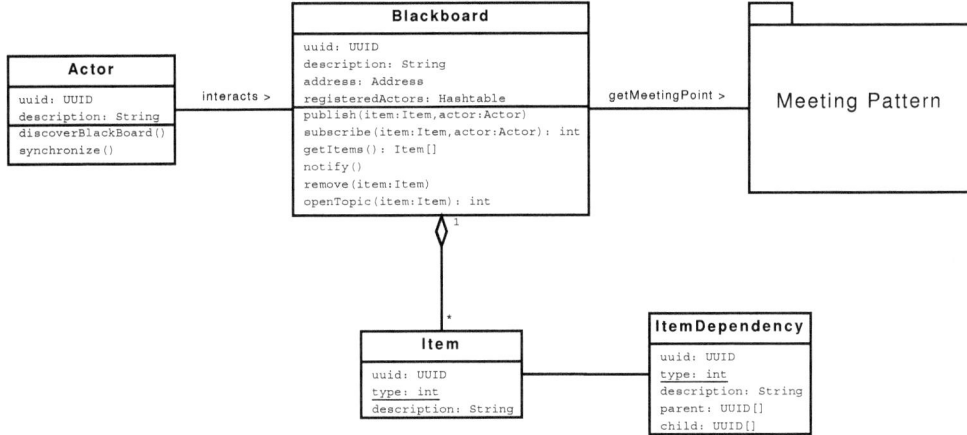

Figure 3.13: Class Diagram of the Blackboard Pattern

interaction is feasible.

Implementation

Figure 3.13 depicts a UML class diagram of the blackboard pattern. An `Actor` can discover a `Blackboard` and start interacting with it. The `Blackboard` can get–if required– a `MeetingPoint` object from the meeting pattern (see Figure 3.12). Moreover, it aggregates `Items` which are associated with `ItemDependency` objects. The `Blackboard` class encapsulates all the necessary logic such as opening topics, publishing or removing items, or subscribing to particular items.

Known Use

This pattern was initially introduced within the field of Artificial Intelligence and agent technology [128]. In [120], publish/subscribe was adopted in mobile environments.

Related Patterns

In [67], the reason for an assignment of the mediator pattern is to separate objects so that they are only aware of the mediator but not of each other, which is very similar to a blackboard. The publish/subscribe messaging paradigm is also availed in the message bus pattern [157] which introduces a bus that knows how to format a message and how to send the message via some channels. The pattern was also investigated in [144].

Negotiating Pattern

Negotiating has initially be scientifically examined in the field of social sciences [78] where among others social choice theory [6] describes how individual preference of agents are aggregated to an election in a voting scenario.

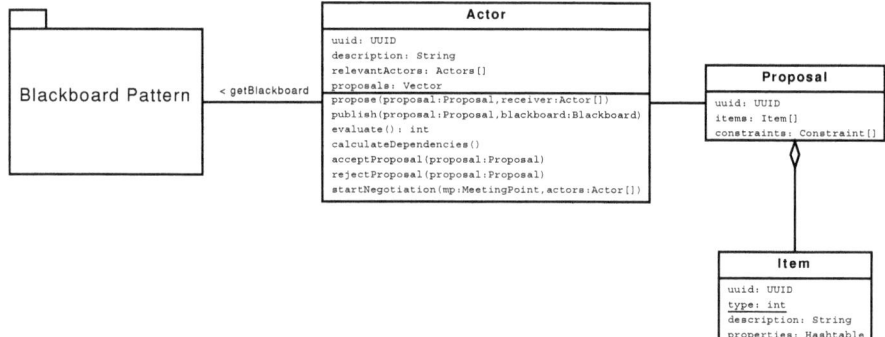

Figure 3.14: Class Diagram of the Negotiation Coordination Pattern

These considerations are basis for many negotiation issues in computer science, too and are strongly related to the *negotiating* pattern.

Context

In many situations, actors in pervasive environments have to cooperate in order to achieve their goal and consequently, provide the user the required service. However, several such actors may have conflicting intentions or may issue conflicting instructions to the environment they are embedded in. Mechanisms shall be in place to identify such conflicts and to solve them in order to accomplish the overall task.

Problem

How can conflicting intentions and activities between equal actors be detected and resolved?

Solution

In order to resolve this, the entities have to make their intentions explicit, first. Usually this is done by publishing a proposal of intended actions. Other entities may react with accepting, rejecting or proposing counter-proposals. Subsequently, both have to evaluate these intentions and have to consider further alternative courses of action. The exchange of proposals and counter-proposals is pursued until consensus is reached or abandoned otherwise.

Implementation

Figure 3.14 depicts a UML class diagram of the negotiation pattern. This pattern may exploit the blackboard pattern to get a `Blackboard` object to be used as a medium for communication with others actors. The central class is the `Actor` class, where each actor decentrally coordinates the `Proposals` such as proposing, rejecting, or accepting. `Proposals` on their part aggregate an arbitrary number of `Item` objects.

Known Use

This type of pattern commonly occurs in social networks. Software agents are often regarded as socially competent. Hence, this sociality of multi-agent systems can be beneficially exploited. The BDI approach

[140] represents such an attempt. For the ultimate purpose of reaching the high-level goal, so called intelligent agents use their social ability to negotiate in order to reach their desires (i.e. individual goals) by exchanging proposals and counter-proposals until a compromise can be agreed on [93].

Related Patterns
In social science as well as in computer science the collective choice theory [62, 156] and voting [129] are strongly related concepts. Also, game theory [65], different interests of actors need to be resolved by negotiations, in order to reach a state of equilibrium (such as a Nash equilibrium [124]). An in-depth study on negotiation patterns and proposal for a negotiation pattern language can be found in [135].

These and other coordination patterns were discussed in detail in [19].

3.2.2 A Formalization of CorA

This Section gives a formal description of the conceptual coordination architecture. This formalization of CorA is exploited in two ways: First, the concepts and mechanisms can structurally be captured and modelled in an abstract sense. Hence, it can be used for abstracting the system a priori, i.e., before implementation. Second, the model and its correctness can be formally verified and state-based reasoning and behaviour estimations can be conducted a posteriori. During the course of this work, a separation in "a priori" formalizing and "a posteriori" reasoning and verification was not adhered. Rather both approaches alternated iteratively, which even resulted in positive effects such that formalization and implementation beneficially influenced each other. As an illustrative example the necessity and integration of version vectors (see Section 3.2.1.4) into CorA was discovered while formally reasoning about the replication strategies and eventually implemented in the architecture.

Several mathematical formalisms would be feasible. One widely used formalisms is the π-calculus [118, 119], which is used to describe processes and communication between processes. Although it was developed more than 15 years ago, it was designed to accommodate mobile processes. Nowadays, mobile computing has progressed and novel properties and requirements have arisen which still can be addressed by the π-calculus. The resulting models, however, may be rather substantial in size and difficult to understand and process. Another calculus is UNITY[25] [37]. UNITY is a formal notation model and proof logic optimised for describing concurrent processes in parallel systems with a focus on simplicity. UNITY has been existing for about 20 year as well. Consequently, the set of original concepts is not sufficient any more. In [114], UNITY has been extended to satisfy the novel requirements and to address mobility potentially in all its forms. The extended version is called *Mobile UNITY*, and refers to a notation system and proof logic designed to accommodate the special needs of the emerging fields of mobile computing. The model allows to define units of computation and mobility and the formal rules for coordination among them in a highly decoupled and opportunistic manner.

Mobile UNITY can be employed as the basis for a formal semantic characterization of coordination models and thus, seems to be suitable for the purpose of modelling CorA, too. The following Subsection 3.2.2.1 introduces the Mobile UNITY notation. This is done by describing already the concrete CorA formalism of distributed tuple spaces and how to interact with them. Subsection 3.2.2.2 formalizes the four replication

---
[25]UNITY stands for "Unbounded Nondeterministic Iterative Transformations"

strategies as introduced in Section 3.2.1.4. Finally, Subsection 3.2.2.3 analyses the costs of each replication strategy in terms of number of necessary tuple transmissions.

3.2.2.1 The Mobile UNITY Notation and CorA's Formal Semantics

This Section introduces the notation of the UNITY formalism and its extension Mobile UNITY. This is accomplished by using two concrete examples of formalizing a program exhibiting the supervisor/worker pattern as introduced in Section 3.2.1.5 in two different ways: deploying *(i)* a centralized (see Figure 3.15) and *(ii)* a decentralized approach (see Figure 3.16). The former approach is very similar to original Linda-like systems mainly for stationary networks and applications. The latter corresponds to the idea of a coordination architecture for pervasive environments as proposed in this work and is presented later. This introduction is self-contained and explains all the concepts necessary for the understanding of the subsequent sections and the formalizations of the replication strategies. For more information and UNITY and Mobile UNITY and related concepts beyond the scope of this work the interested reader is referred to either [37] or [142, 143].

The basic idea of this example is that a supervisor injects tasks as tuples into a tuple space called `taskSpace`—be it a centralized or a decentralized one. Workers can according to their capabilities take tasks out, complete them, and eventually insert them again. Finally, the supervisor can access the final result represented by all completed tasks.

To understand a Mobile UNITY program we first start with explaining the general structure: A **System** contains one or more **Programs**. The **Components** section describes all the instances which are composed together by the union operator ⦅. The **Interactions** section defines the behaviour of the mobile components when connected. The **Program** section has three further sections: the **declare** section, where variables are declared in a Pascal-like fashion. A variable declared by additionally using the **coop** keyword is called a shared variable because it can be read and written by other connected programs in a transient way. The **initially** section defines initial values and constraints of variables. The program's actions (i.e., state transitions) are defined in the **assign** section. These assignments are usually conditional or guarded, respectively. Assignments are separated by the ⦅ sign. In particular, they can also be separated by a ∥ denoting that the two separated assignments are executed in the same atomic step. The execution of each UNITY program—and, thus, also of each Mobile UNITY program—starts in a state satisfying the initial constraints defined in the **initially** section. The statements to be executed in each step are selected non-deterministically in a "weakly fair manner" [37], i.e., each statement is scheduled for execution infinitely often in an infinite computation (where all computations are infinite). If a statement is selected its condition is examined and if true it is executed. Each executed statement produces an atomic transformation of the program state.

It is important to mention that the presented examples are placed in the context of mobile environments (thus, location is essential) in order to allow for comparability. The mobile components (i.e., programs) can only communicate if they are connected. In all subsequent Mobile UNITY programs, λ denotes a location where the representation of the concrete location is entirely dependent on the application. Hence, location could be a physical location such as GPS coordinates in a specific geographic reference model (such as, for instance, WGS84) or a symbolic location (such as an URI like `salzburgresearch.at/location`). λ can dynamically change during runtime. Connectivity between mobile peers is expressed by the symmetric and transitive relation

κ. The predicate a κ b denotes that both peers' proximity (a and b) is close enough such that they are within range and can communicate with each other and exchange data. In other words a κ b $\equiv$ a.λ = b.λ.

The program shown in Figure 3.15[26] describes a centralized supervisor/worker solution (like in the original Linda system). This example subsumes four components: the central tuple space, one supervisor and two workers. The central tuple space contains a `taskSpace` which is transiently sharable (**coop** keyword). The supervisor as well as the worker contain tuples representing tasks and results. Additionally, the worker holds a variable describing his capability. In Line 12, Figure 3.15 φ is assigned to the `result` variable, where φ stands for a tuple template containing formals.

If the predicate `taskAvailable`[27] holds true then the supervisor creates a task tuple by invoking the function `createTaskTuple()` which is specified as[28]

$$\langle \| \; i : 0 \leq i < N :: task[i] := taskInfo[i] \rangle$$

where `N` is the number of available tasks and `taskInfo[i]` contains information about the `ith` task which is populated from any source outside the system considered here (e.g., possibly injected by any user application such as any appropriate GUI for task definition). The task is inserted into the tuple space `taskSpace` iff a κ b as specified in the **Interactions** section. Mobile UNITY also supports the concept of namespaces to uniquely address variables. For instance, to access the variable `taskSpace` the construct `b.taskSpace` is used where `b` is an element of the $\mathcal{TS}$ set subsuming tuple spaces. ($\mathcal{C}$ is the set of clients (here supervisors and workers) interacting with the central tuple space contained in $\mathcal{TS}$.) The sharing construct $\approx$ defines the symmetrical and transitive sharing of variables that belong to different programs (in Line 33 of Figure 3.15 the client a accesses the variable `tasksSpace` of the tuple space b via the concept of namespaces).

After insertion of the tasks by the supervisor by invoking the `out()` function it keeps on retrieving results following an **unless** relation which is defined as [37]

$$p \; unless \; q \equiv \langle \forall a : a \in P :: \{p \land \neg q\} \; a \; \{p \lor q\} \rangle$$

where `p` and `q` are states, a is an action and `P` a UNITY program. In principle, the notation $\{p\} \; a \; \{q\}$ is the standard Hoare-triple notation [82] saying that the action a results in a state change from `p` to `q`. Thus, the **unless** relation describes that if `p` holds at some point in the computation and `q` does not, in the next step `p` remains true or `q` becomes true. Hence, if `p` is true at any point during the execution of `P` then either `q` never holds and `p` continues to hold forever, or `q` holds eventually and `p` continues to hold at least until `q` holds.

---

[26] To improve readability, in the following examples we present Mobile UNITY keywords in bold font (like **assign**), functions and predicates are in typewriter font (like `createTaskTuple()`), comments are in italics and curly brackets (like $\{Send\}$), the tuple fields—in CorA the W5 fields—are in capitals (like WHATABOUT), field-variables are in small capitals (like REPLSTRAT) separated with a dot from the W5 field, and constants are in capitals too (like FULL_PUSH).

[27] For brevity's sake, obvious and trivial predicates and functions are not further formally specified.

[28] The three-part notation $\langle operator \; variables : range\_constraint :: expression \rangle$ used throughout this work is defined as follows: The variables from *variables* take on all possible values permitted by *range_constraint*. If *range_constraint* is missing, the first colon is omitted and the domain of the variables is restricted by context. Each such instantiation of the variables is substituted in expression producing a multiset of values to which *operator* is applied, yielding the value of the three-part expression. If no instantiation of the *variables* satisfies *range_constraint*, the value of the three-part expression is the identity element for *operator*, e.g., *true* if *operator* is $\forall$.

The worker first invokes the function `getCapability()`. Then it keeps on retrieving tuples from the space invoking the `in()` function unless `tupleMatchesTemplate` does not hold, which is defined as

$$\texttt{tupleMatchesTemplate} \equiv \langle \exists \tau : \tau \in \mathcal{T}_{\mathcal{TS}} :: \mathcal{M}(\tau, \varphi) \rangle$$

The operation $\mathcal{M}(\tau, \varphi)$ was first defined in [123] and is applied here too. It formally expresses that a tuple τ matches a template φ. $\mathcal{T}_{\mathcal{TS}}$ comprises all tuples contained in tuple space $\mathcal{TS}$.

A task is executed (invoking `execute(task)`) iff `capabilityMatches` holds. The obtained result is inserted into the tuple space by `out()`.

The basic space operations `out(Tuple` τ`)`, `in(Template` φ`)`, and `in_all(Template` φ`)` are specified as:

$$\texttt{out}(\tau) \equiv \mathcal{TS} := \mathcal{TS} \cup \tau$$

$$\texttt{in}(\varphi) \equiv \langle \exists \tau : \tau \in \mathcal{TS} \wedge \mathcal{M}(\tau, \varphi) :: \mathcal{TS} := \mathcal{TS} \setminus \{\tau\} \rangle$$

$$\texttt{in\_all}(\varphi) \equiv \langle \| \ \forall \tau : \tau \in \mathcal{TS} \wedge \mathcal{M}(\tau, \varphi) :: \mathcal{TS} := \mathcal{TS} \setminus \{\tau\} \rangle$$

In the program of Figure 3.15 the space operations `out()`, `in()`, and `in_all()` are all used with only one argument: the tuple that needs to be processed. This is because there is only one central space present and the interaction with it is implicitly clear. In all other and subsequent Mobile UNITY programs multiple spaces are available. Hence, these examples use variants of the formalized space operations that are equal but introduce a second argument: the tuple space on which the specified tuple has to be processed. The signatures of the functions are `out(TupleSpace` $\mathcal{TS}$, `Tuple` τ`)`, `in(TupleSpace` $\mathcal{TS}$, `Template` φ`)`, and `in_all(TupleSpace` $\mathcal{TS}$, `Template` φ`)`. The same is true for the `read()` and `read_all()` operation which is also used in the following Mobile UNITY programs and is formally defined very similar to `in()` and `in_all()`. The differences— as introduced in Section 3.2.1.3—is merely that `read()` is non-destructive and leaves the read tuples in the space and does not remove any tuples.

As argued earlier, CorA deploys multiple distributed tuple spaces (as also supported in [70] and [87]) locally available on each involved peer. The second Mobile UNITY program example (presented in Figure 3.16) formalizes this approach and highlights the main difference to the first example with a central tuple space (Figure 3.15).

The most obvious difference is inherent to the peer-to-peer based approach in contrast to a classic client/server set-up: Now, there is just one program called **Peer**, which can be distinguished through an identifier. Hence, all peers are equal but have different roles; easily one **Worker** can transform itself into a **Supervisor** and vice versa. Instead of the four instantiated components as in the program of Figure 3.15, there are now only three peers where each one has a unique identifier, which are **Supervisor**, **Worker1**, and **Worker2**. The central tuple space component is missing. Instead, each peer carries a portion of the tuple space. These portions are "joined" upon connectivity between the mobile peers.

```
 1  System SupervisorWorker_centralized
      Program CentralTupleSpace at λ
 3      declare
          taskSpace : coop TupleSpace
 5      initially
          taskSpace = {}
 7    end
      Program Supervisor at λ
 9      declare
          task, result : Tuple
11      initially
          task = {} ⫿ result = φ
13      assign
          task := createTaskTuple()       if taskAvailable
15      ⫿ out(task)
        ⫿ result := in_all(result)   unless ¬resultAvailable
17    end
      Program Worker(identifier) at λ
19      declare
          task, result : Tuple
21        capability : Capability
        initially
23        task = φ ⫿ result = {} ⫿ capability = {}
        assign
25        capability := getCapability()
        ⫿ task := in(task)        unless ¬tupleMatchesTemplate
27      ⫿ result := execute(task)    if capabilityMatches
        ⫿ out(result)      if taskCompleted
29    end
      Components
31      CentralTupleSpace ⫿ Supervisor ⫿ Worker(1) ⫿ Worker(2)
      Interactions
33      ⟨∀a,b : a ∈ C, b ∈ TS :: a ≈ b.taskSpace
                              when a κ b ⟩
35  end
```

Figure 3.15: A centralized Supervisor/Worker Mobile UNITY Program

```
 1  System SupervisorWorker_decentralized
      Program Peer(identifier) at λ
 3      declare
          taskSpace, adminSpace : TupleSpace
 5        address, task, result : Tuple
          capability : Capability
 7      initially
          taskSpace = {} [] adminSpace = {}
 9        [] address = {} [] task = {} [] result = {}
          [] capability = {}
11      assign
          address := getPeerAddress()
13        [] out(adminSpace, address)
          [] capability := getCapability()
15        [] task := createTaskTuple()     if taskAvailable
          [] out(taskSpace, task)
17        [] task := in(taskSpace, task)   unless ¬tupleMatchesTemplate
                                           ∧ if capabilityMatches
19        [] result := execute(task)
          [] out(taskSpace, result)        unless ¬taskCompleted
21        [] result := in_all(taskSpace, result)   unless ¬resultAvailable
        end
23      Components
          Peer(Supervisor) [] Peer(Worker1) [] Peer(Worker2)
25      Interactions
          ⟨∀a,b : a,b ∈ P :: a κ b⟩
27        {Copy address tuple to addressSpaces}
          [] ⟨∀a,b : a,b ∈ P :: a.adminSpace ≈ b.adminSpace
29                                 when a κ b
                                   reactsTo adminSpaceEvent⟩
31        {Copy task tuples to taskSpaces}
          [] ⟨[]∀a,b : a,b ∈ P ::
33           ⟨|| i : 0 ≤ i < a.taskSpace.size() :: a.taskSpace ≈ b.taskSpace
                                   when a κ b
35                                 reactsTo taskSpaceEvent⟩
          ⟩
37        {Copy results to taskSpaces}
          [] ⟨∀a,b : a,b ∈ P :: a.taskSpace ≈ b.taskSpace
39                                 when a κ b
                                   reactsTo resultEvent⟩
41  end
```

Figure 3.16: A De-centralized Supervisor/Worker Mobile UNITY Program

As a consequence to this different set-up the involved peers do not have a central contact point to get administrative data, such as addresses of and communication channels to other peers. This is resolved by introducing besides the `taskSpace` also a distributed `adminSpace` that holds such address information. By first invoking the `getPeerAddress()` function a peer collects all the relevant addresses of peers in range and by executing `out()` in Line 13 the corresponding address tuples are stored in the `adminSpace`. The remainder of the program is very similar to the centralized example but everything is covered now by only one program. The **Interactions** is different: All nodes (i.e., peers) are now subsumed by the set $\mathcal{P}$. The formalized interactions are more complex, too. Line 26 describes basic connectivity equal to the one already introduced in example 3.15. Line 28 describes the interactions necessary as a reaction (**reactsTo** directive) after an `adminSpaceEvent` occurred. In CorA, events can be registered that condition a subsequent reaction. Such an `adminSpaceEvent` could be the request of transmission of address tuples (on the receiver's side) or also the arrival of requested addresses (on the sender's side). This is very similar for a `taskSpaceEvent` dealing with submitted or modified task tuples in the `taskSpace` (see Line 32) or a `resultEvent` denoting the availability of results (Line 38).

Clearly, the centralized approach seems to be more straightforward and, in fact, is easier to implement, is shorter in length, and requires less effort, which is directly reflected in source code. However, it is also clear that all the drawbacks as argued in Section 3.2.1.3 are inherent to the presented centralized solution. The decentralized solution exploiting distributed tuple spaces requires more functionality encapsulated within a communication infrastructure or middleware in order to guarantee an improved system behaviour confronted to the centralized solution.

3.2.2.2 Tuple Replication Semantics

In this Section we formally describe the four replication strategies provided by CorA which were introduced in Section 3.2.1.4 (see also Figure 3.9):

1. Full Replication – Push (I)
2. Full Replication – Pull (II)
3. Context-dependent Replication – Pull (III)
4. Context-dependent Replication – Push (IV)

The proceeding sections deal with each strategy in more detail and formally describe them.

Full Replication – Push (I)

The full replication strategy in push mode (I) is characterised by the fact that one or more produced tuples are sent from one peer to all currently connected peers. After an examination whether a duplicate tuple is already present at the remote peer the tuple(s) is/are stored accordingly there. Otherwise all fields of a present tuple are updated according to the new values. This strategy usually is the reaction to an event. A simple example of such an event might be that one peer creates a new W5 tuple containing information relevant for the whole peer

```
 1  System SupervisorWorker_replication_FULL_PUSH
      Program Peer(identifier) at λ
 3      declare
          taskSpace : TupleSpace
 5        task : Tuple
        initially
 7        taskSpace = {} ⟦ task = {}
        assign
 9        {Send}
          task := createTaskTuple()
11      ⟦ [WHATABOUT.REPLSTRAT:FULL_PUSH] ⊕ task
        ⟦ out(taskSpace, task)
13      ∥ executeReplication()
          {Receive}
15      ⟦ out(taskSpace, prepareUpdatedTuple(task))   if tupleReceivedEvent
                                                      ∧ ¬duplicatePresent
17      end
        Components
19        Peer(0) ⟦ Peer(1) ⟦ ... ⟦ Peer(n)
        Interactions
21        ⟨∀a,b : a,b ∈ P :: a κ b⟩
          {Update tuples in receiver's taskSpace}
23      ⟦ ⟨⟦∀s,r,τ : s,r ∈ P ∧ τ ∈ T ::
             ⟨∥ i : 0 ≤ i < |T| :: s.taskSpace ≈ r.taskSpace
25                               ∧ r.taskspace := r.taskspace + τ
                                 when s κ r
27                               reactsTo tupleReceivedEvent⟩
          ⟩
29   end
```

Figure 3.17: The Full-Push Replication Strategy (I)

group which was not yet present in that form. Related to the chosen supervisor/worker scenario a supervisor peer creates a new task tuple. Prior to storing it in its local `taskSpace`, this peer sets the relevant value in the *Whatabout* field (see also Section 3.2.1.2). In the related Mobile UNITY program in Figure 3.17 this is done in Line 11 by the statement

$$[\text{WHATABOUT.REPLSTRAT:FULL\_PUSH}] \oplus \text{task}$$

which is the Mobile UNITY notation used to assign values to fields.

In addition to the program code of this replication strategy, Figure 3.18 illustrates the sequence of actions by using a UML Sequence diagram.

It is important to mention that replication is done in the same atomic step as the insertion of tuples into the local space (indicated by the ∥ sign in Line 13). The **Components** section shows that an arbitrary number of peers can exist. In the **Interactions** section this is addressed by the set P subsuming all peers and the set T combining all tuples. The `tupleReceivedEvent` triggers reactions in the peers. The predicate `duplicatePresent` is evaluated first. It is examined whether the same tuple is already present. If so the newly received tuple is discarded if not the function `prepareUpdatedTuple()` is executed and the updated tuple is inserted to the corresponding space via `out()`.

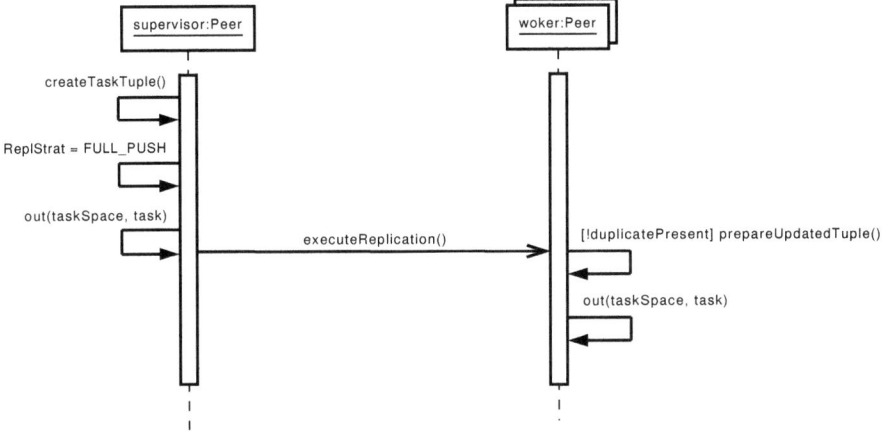

Figure 3.18: Sequence of Actions in Full-Push

Iff duplicatePresent is false means that no equal tuple is present in the space and hence, the new one can be inserted. duplicatePresent is defined as

duplicatePresent $\equiv false$ iff
$\langle [\!] \sharp \tau_0 : \tau_0 \in \mathcal{T} ::$
$\quad \langle \| \ i, \tau : 0 \leq i < |\mathcal{T}| \wedge \tau \in \mathcal{T} ::$
$\quad \quad \tau_0.\text{WHATABOUT.UUID} = \tau.\text{WHATABOUT.UUID}$
$\quad \quad \wedge \mathcal{VV}(\tau_0, \tau) \rangle$
$\rangle$

where UUID represents a universally unique identifier kept in the *Whatabout* field. The predicate $\mathcal{VV}(\tau_0, \tau)$ is defined as

$\mathcal{VV}(\tau_0, \tau) \equiv true$ iff
$\quad |\tau_0.\text{WHATABOUT.}VV| = |\tau.\text{WHATABOUT.}VV|$
$\quad \wedge \langle \| \ i : 0 \leq i < |\mathcal{T}| :: \tau_0.\text{WHATABOUT.}VV.key[i] = \tau.\text{WHATABOUT.}VV.key[i] \rangle$
$\quad \wedge \langle \| \ i : 0 \leq i < |\mathcal{T}| :: \tau_0.\text{WHATABOUT.}VV.value[i] = \tau.\text{WHATABOUT.}VV.value[i] \rangle$

where VV represents the version vector which is stored in the meta information field (i.e., *Whatabout*) of W5 tuples. Version vectors in CorA comprise a key and a value field (similar to a hash-table construct), where the key contains addresses of peers that modified the tuple and each value related to a key contains a list of timestamps when these modifications happened.

The function prepareUpdatedTuple() "combines" the newly received tuple with the one already present in the space, determines the more recent one with the latest modifications, conducts adaptations if necessary, and finally provides *one* synthesized tuple to out(). This final tuple is inserted into the relevant space. This

```
 1  System SupervisorWorker_replication_FULL_PULL
 2    Program Peer(identifier) at λ
        declare
 4        taskSpace : TupleSpace
          task, request : Tuple
 6      initially
          taskSpace = {} ⌈ task = {} ⌈ request = {}
 8      assign
          {Send}
10        request := createTaskTuple()
          ⌈ [WHATABOUT.REPLSTRAT:FULL_PULL] ⊕ request
12        ⌈ out(taskSpace, request)
          ‖ executeReplication()
14        {Receive}
          ⌈ task := read_all(taskSpace, request)    if requestReceivedEvent
16                                                ∧ unless ¬tupleMatchesTemplate
          ‖ sendToPeer(task)
18     end
       Components
20       Peer(0) ⌈ Peer(1) ⌈ ... ⌈ Peer(n)
       Interactions
22       ⟨∀a,b : a,b ∈ P :: a κ b⟩
         {Insert request tuples into receiver's taskSpace}
24     ⌈ ⟨⌈∀s,r,τ : s,r ∈ P ∧ τ ∈ T ::
              ⟨‖ i : 0 ≤ i < |T| :: s.taskSpace ≈ r.taskSpace
26                              ∧ r.taskspace := r.taskspace + τ
                                when s κ r
28                              reactsTo requestReceivedEvent⟩
         ⟩
30     end
```

Figure 3.19: The Full-Pull Replication Strategy (II)

sequence is also illustrated in Figure 3.18.

Full Replication – Pull (II)

The full replication strategy in pull mode (II) is characterised by the fact that peers can explicitly and on demand ask other peers for one or more tuples which are then transferred to the querying peers. An example of such a case might be that a new peer joins a network or a peer group and first requests all address tuples representing the connected peers from an **adminSpace** of another peer.

Figure 3.19 depicts the corresponding Mobile UNITY program. There are two main differences in this program with respect to the first full replication strategy in push mode: First, the strategy has to be set accordingly to FULL_PULL in the *Whatabout* field. Second, the **requestReceivedEvent** as a new type of event is introduced to which the receiver reacts (see Line 15 of Figure 3.19). As a consequence to this event the receiver reads all tuples of its local space matching the template tuple **request** that was submitted together with the sender's query. After that the function **sendToPeer()** with the relevant tuples as arguments is invoked to deliver the required information to the requester.

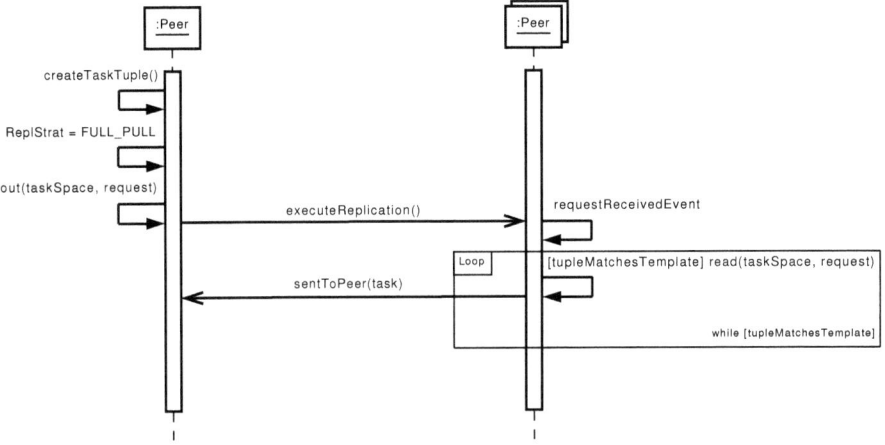

Figure 3.20: Sequence of Actions in Full-Pull

Figure 3.20 shows this process in form of a UML Sequence diagram.

Context-dependent Replication – Pull (III)

In the context-dependent replication strategy in pull mode (III) peers can—depending on the described context—request specific (i.e., context-dependent) information encapsulated in tuples. The described context does not necessarily have to be their current context but can be any context which is relevant. The context is described by the fields of the W5 model, hence in principle to four dimensions (actor, activity, space, and time) plus meta-information. The Mobile UNITY program of this replication strategy is very similar to the full-pull strategy of Figure 3.19. Figure 3.21 introduces the new parts without repeating the already presented code fragments.

In Line 21 the replication strategy is defined: CONTEXT_PULL. The code from Line 23 onwards defines the definition of various context parameters; here exemplified: a position defined by longitude and latitude (by using the *Where* field of W5), and a time frame defined by a begin time and an end time (by using the *When* field of W5). Also the sequence of actions is very similar to the one of the full-pull strategy and shall not be repeated (see also Figure 3.20).

```
System SupervisorWorker_replication_CONTEXT_PULL
2    Program Peer( identifier ) at λ
        declare
4          { Like the FULL_PULL strategy }
        initially
6          { Like the FULL_PULL strategy }
        assign
8          { Send }
           request := createTaskTuple()
10         ⫿ [WHATABOUT. REPLSTRAT :CONTEXT_PULL]  ⊕  request
           { Define the context, e.g.: }
12         ⫿ [WHERE. POSITION:{ longitude , latitude }] ⊕ request
           ⫿ [WHEN. TIMEFRAME :{ beginTime , endTime }] ⊕ request
14         {...}
           ⫿ out(taskSpace , request)
16         ∥ executeReplication()
           { Receive }
18         { Remainder is like the FULL_PULL strategy }
           {...}
20
        end
```

Figure 3.21: The Context-dependent-Pull Replication Strategy (III)

Context-dependent Replication – Push (IV)

The context-dependent replication strategy in push mode (IV) allows peers to subscribe to events and to get required fields of tuples event-based and in a context-dependent way. The subscribers define the event, the particular context, and the information (contained in fields) they are interested in. The peers that can provide such information and listen to the requested events deliver this information as pushed tuples as soon as an event during the defined context happens. Figure 3.22 introduces the corresponding Mobile UNITY program.

The code from Line 11 to Line 15 describes how a peer can create a tuple that can be exploited for subscription to particular events (local as well as remote). The definition of context parameters is similar as in the program of Figure 3.21. Implicitly, this involves two issues combined in one atomic step: First, a peer can describe the context of interest and, second, the peer can define which information about this context must be returned. This particular procedure was one further outcome of the formal reasoning approach in defining the replication strategies. The concrete implementations based on this reasoning—also regarding this particular case—can be found in Section 3.3. The **eventSpace** is introduced as a further tuple space available on each peer, to which this **subscribe** tuple is eventually inserted (Line 17). As soon as a **subscriptionReceivedEvent** fires at any peer, it inserts this **subscribe** tuple into its **eventSpace** and registers an according listener. If an event occurs (Line 31) the peer examines its **eventSpace**, takes out all relevant **subscribe** tuples, creates the related tuples and inserts them into the **taskSpace**. As mentioned earlier in the section about the full-push (I) strategy, the space operation **out()** is internally one atomic step together with the replication functions. Hence, by invoking **out()** (in Line 32) the tuple is locally inserted but also distributed to all other peers registered for that event in that particular context (as defined before in the **subscribe** tuple). These remote peers, in turn, are notified by a **tupleReceivedEvent**. Again the UML Sequence diagram of Figure 3.23 should help to better visualize the ongoing actions.

```
1  System SupervisorWorker_replication_CONTEXT_PUSH
     Program Peer(identifier) at λ
3      declare
         taskSpace, eventSpace : TupleSpace
5        task, request, subscribe : Tuple
       initially
7        taskSpace = {} ⫾ eventSpace = {}
         ⫾ task = {} ⫾ request = {} ⫾ subscribe = {}
9      assign
         {Subscribe}
11       subscribe := createTaskTuple()
         ⫾ [WHATABOUT. REPLSTRAT:CONTEXT_PUSH] ⊕ subscribe
13       {Define the context, e.g.:}
         ⫾ [WHERE. POSITION:{longitude, latitude}] ⊕ subscribe
15       ⫾ [WHEN. TIMEFRAME:{beginTime, endTime}] ⊕ subscribe
         {...}
17       ⫾ out(eventSpace, subscribe)
         ∥ executeReplication()
19       {Send}
         request := createTaskTuple()
21       ⫾ [WHATABOUT. REPLSTRAT:CONTEXT_PULL] ⊕ request
         {Define the context, e.g.:}
23       ⫾ [WHERE. POSITION:{longitude, latitude}] ⊕ request
         ⫾ [WHEN. TIMEFRAME:{beginTime, endTime}] ⊕ request
25       {...}
         ⫾ out(taskSpace, request)
27       {Receive}
         ⫾ out(eventSpace, subscribe) if subscriptionReceivedEvent
29       ⫾ out(taskSpace, task) if tupleReceivedEvent
         {Event occurs}
31       ⫾ task := in_all(eventSpace, subscribe) unless ¬tupleMatchesTemplate
         ⫾ out(taskSpace, task)
33     end
       Components
35       Peer(0) ⫾ Peer(1) ⫾ ... ⫾ Peer(n)
       Interactions
37       ⟨∀a,b : a,b ∈ 𝒫 :: a κ b⟩
         {Insert request tuples into receiver's taskSpace}
39     ⫾ ⟨⫾∀s,r,τ : s,r ∈ 𝒫 ∧ τ ∈ 𝒯 ::
             ⟨∥ i : 0 ≤ i < |𝒯| :: s.taskSpace ≈ r.taskSpace
41                              ∧ r.taskspace := r.taskspace + τ
                                when s κ r
43                              reactsTo subscriptionReceivedEvent⟩
         ⟩
45     ⫾ ⟨⫾∀s,r,τ : s,r ∈ 𝒫 ∧ τ ∈ 𝒯 ::
             ⟨∥ i : 0 ≤ i < |𝒯| :: r.taskSpace ≈ s.taskSpace
47                              ∧ r.taskspace := s.taskspace + τ
                                when r κ s
49                              reactsTo tupleReceivedEvent⟩
         ⟩
51 end
```

Figure 3.22: The Context-dependent-Push Replication Strategy (IV)

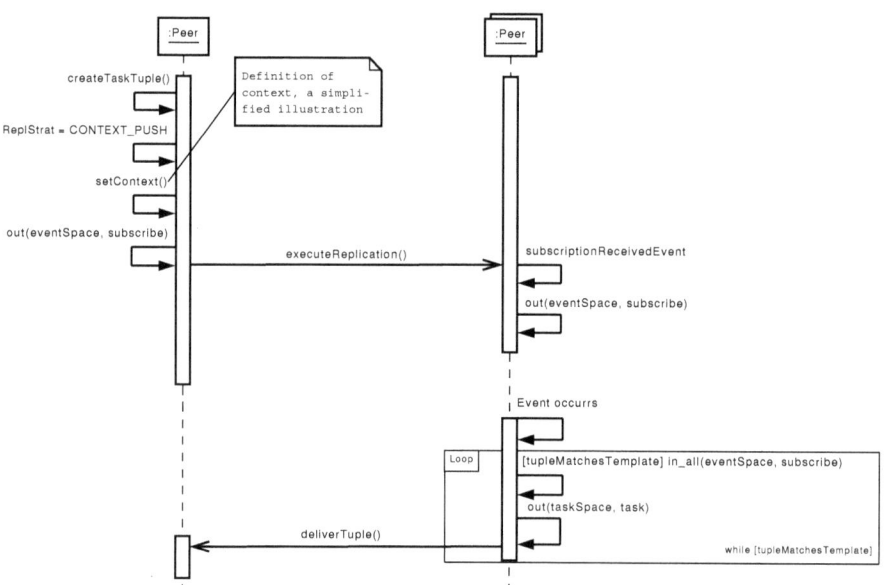

Figure 3.23: Sequence of Actions in Context-dependent-Push

3.2.2.3 Replication Costs

According to the formalizations of the four replication strategies the following "costs" in terms of necessary tuple transmissions T can be determined as described in the following formulas. Formula 3.1 specifies the number of transmission T_I necessary for the full-push strategy

$$T_I = N \cdot (N\tau - \tau) \tag{3.1}$$

where N is the total number of available peers in a peer group and τ is the number of tuple transmissions.

Formula 3.2 specifies the number of transmission T_{II} necessary for the full-pull strategy

$$T_{II} = \sum_{i=1}^{N} N_C \cdot (1 + \tau_\varphi) \tag{3.2}$$

where N_C is the total number of *contacted* peers with $N_C \leq (N-1)$ and τ_φ stands for all tuples τ matching the template φ.

Formula 3.3 specifies the number of transmission T_{III} necessary for the context-dependent-pull strategy

$$T_{III} \equiv T_{II} \; where \; |T_{III}| \leq |T_{II}| \tag{3.3}$$

where T_{III} is always less than or equal to T_{II} because $\tau_{\varphi(III)} \subseteq \tau_{\varphi(II)}$ where τ_φ represents the number of tuples τ matching the template φ.

Formula 3.4 specifies the number of transmission T_{IV} necessary for the context-dependent-push strategy

$$T_{IV} = \sum_{i=1}^{N} \left[N_{Ci} \cdot r_i + \sum_{j=1}^{E_i} \tau_\varphi \right] \tag{3.4}$$

where N is the total number of available peers in the peer group and r_i is the number of registrations per peer. E is the total number of firing events for which peers are registered and E_i is the number of firing events at peer i. τ_φ is as above the number of matching tuples.

3.3 Coordination Language Implementation

This Section provides details about the concrete implementation of the coordination architecture CorA, conceptually introduced in the preceding Chapter 3.2. The resulting "linguistic embodiment" of a coordination architecture is referred to as a coordination language [72].

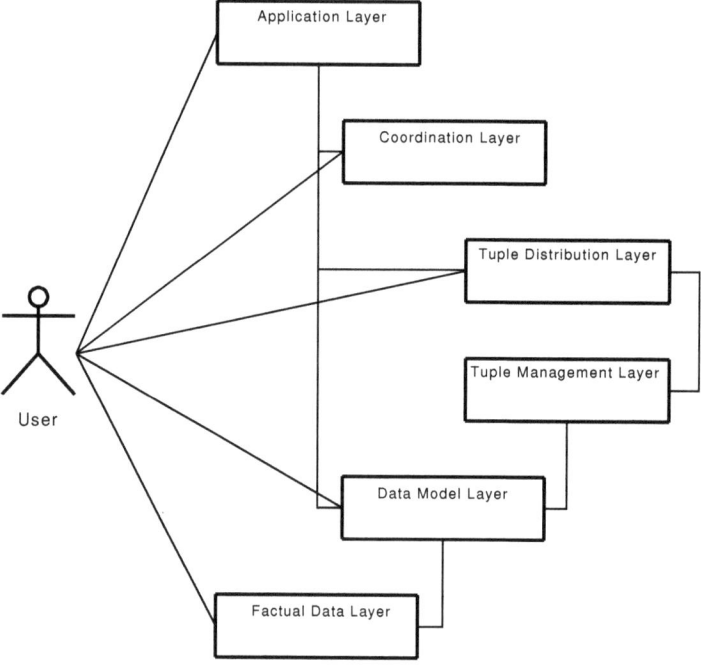

Figure 3.24: Overview of Use Case Diagrams

The Chapter covers the system use cases addressed by CorA (Section 3.3.1), the software system design (Section 3.3.2), details about internal and business logics (Section 3.3.3), and essential usages of the CorA middleware API (Section 3.3.4).

3.3.1 System Use Case Descriptions

This Section provides details about the system use cases covered by CorA. For this, Figure 3.24 gives a high-level overview about the interplay of the various use cases related to the layers of the coordination architecture. Each box represents a use case sub-system or a layer of CorA. The user as actor can directly interact with the application, coordination, tuple distribution, data model, and factual data layer. A detailed use case diagram is provided for each of these sub-systems.

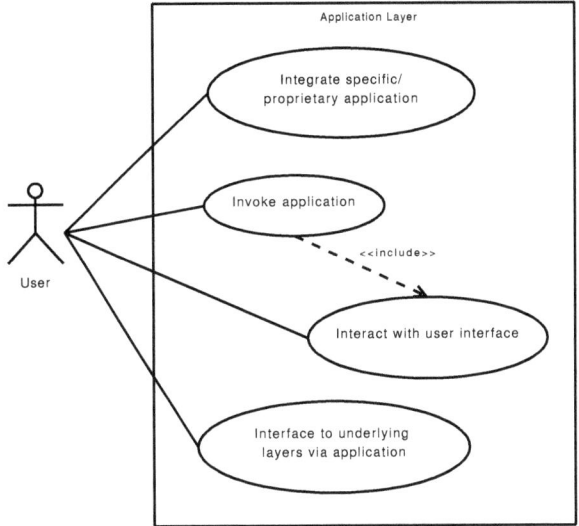

Figure 3.25: Application Layer: Use Case Diagram

Use Case	Description
Integrate specific/proprietary application	On the application layer, applications can be deployed that exploit the underlying CorA middleware.
Invoke application	Actors can invoke such applications.
Interact with user interface	Actors can interact with such applications via user interfaces.
Interface to underlying layers via application	This sub-system embodies interfaces to underlying layers of CorA.

Table 3.5: Application Layer: Detailed Use Case Description

Application Layer Use Cases

Figure 3.25 gives details about the use cases relevant for the application layer of CorA. The only actor for this sub-system is the user. Table 3.5 lists the use cases and gives short descriptions on each.

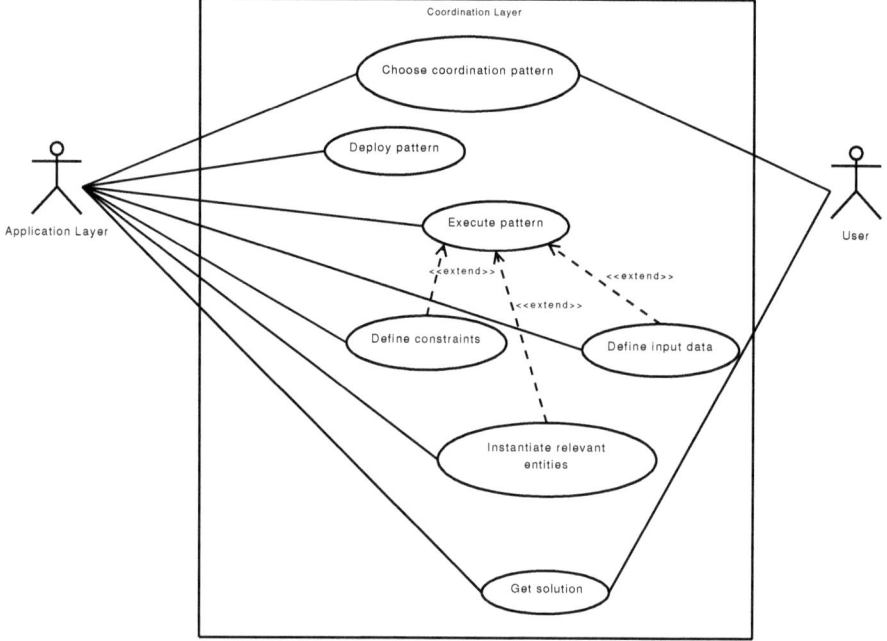

Figure 3.26: Coordination Layer: Use Case Diagram

Coordination Layer Use Cases

Two types of actors can be identified for the use cases related to the coordination layer: the user and the application layer sub-system. Figure 3.26 depicts these use cases and actors and Table 3.6 lists them together with short descriptions.

Tuple Distribution Layer Use Cases

The tuple distribution layer has the same actors as the coordination layer but in addition also the coordination layer sub-system represents one actor. Figure 3.27 and Table 3.7 represent the according use case information. Figure 3.27 shows four derived replication strategies which are pre-defined in CorA and formalized and extensively discussed in Section 3.2.2. Replication strategies are extendable in CorA.

Use Case	Description
Choose coordination pattern	The actors can select various coordination patterns which seem to be most appropriate for solving their problem.
Deploy pattern	The pattern can be deployed as recommended by the pattern catalogue.
Execute pattern	The pattern can be executed in this subsystem which may be extended by the related use cases (see Figure 3.26).
Define constraints	In order to execute a pattern, constraints can be defined.
Define input data	Input data to a pattern can be explicitly defined.
Instantiate relevant entities	For the pattern execution relevant entities can be instantiated.
Get solution	The solution to the coordination problem determined by the pattern can be retrieved.

Table 3.6: Coordination Layer: Detailed Use Case Description

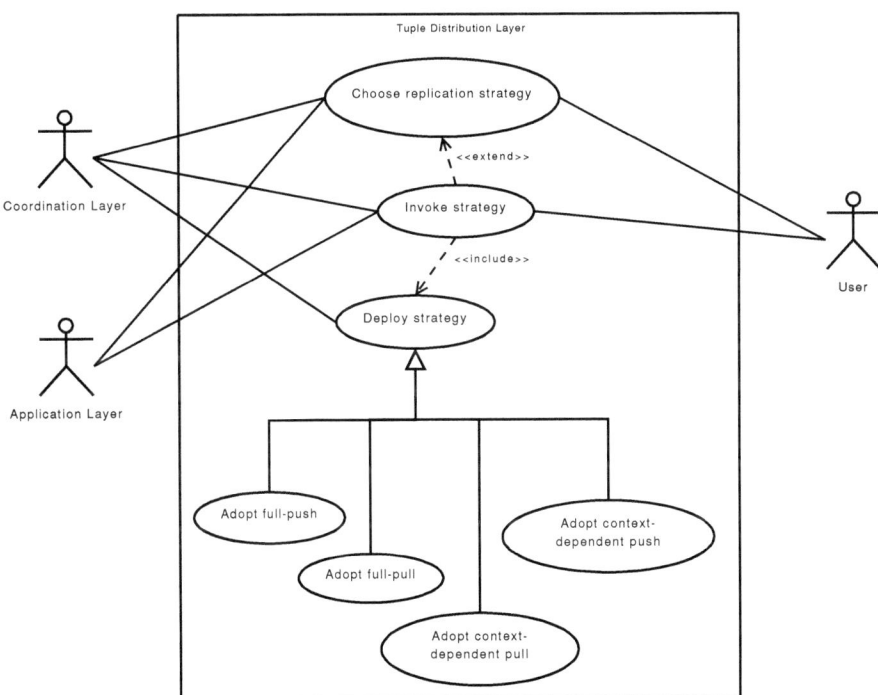

Figure 3.27: Tuple Distribution Layer: Use Case Diagram

Use Case	Description
Choose replication strategy	The actors can choose among diverse replication strategies.
Invoke strategy	The strategy can be invoked, which includes correct deployment.
Deploy strategy	Necessary preconditions can be provided in order to execute a strategy.
Adopt full-push	The full-push strategy can be adopted.
Adopt context-dependent push	The context-dependent-push strategy can be adopted.
Adopt full-pull	The full-pull strategy can be adopted.
Adopt context-dependent pull	The context-dependent pull strategy can be adopted.

Table 3.7: Tuple Distribution Layer: Detailed Use Case Description

Use Case	Description
Insert tuple into space	An actor can insert a tuple into a space.
Insert multiple	Multiple tuples can be inserted with one operation.
Check duplicates	In insertion operation causes a check whether duplicate tuples are already present in the space.
Update Tuple	If a duplicate tuple is presented this can be updated.
Read tuple	An actor can read a tuple without deleting it from the space.
Read multiple	Multiple tuples can be read with one operation.
Delete tuple	An actor can delete a tuple from the space.
Delete multiple	Multiple tuples can be deleted with one operation.
Get matching tuples	Read and delete operations include a determination of matching tuples.

Table 3.8: Tuple Management Layer: Detailed Use Case Description

Tuple Management Layer Use Cases

The only actor interacting with this sub-system is the tuple distribution layer. Figure 3.28 and Table 3.8 give details about this sub-system.

Data Model Layer Use Cases

Figure 3.29 shows the four actors of the data model sub-system: user, application, coordination, and tuple management. Table 3.9 provides details about each use case.

Use Case	Description
Create W5 tuple	Actors can create W5 tuples.
Modify W5 tuple	Actors can access and modify a created W5 Tuple.
Modify fields	The relevant fields can be modified as needed.
Modify WHO	The WHO field can be accessed separately.
Modify WHAT	The WHAT field can be accessed separately.
Modify WHERE	The WHERE field can be accessed separately.
Modify WHEN	The WHEN field can be accessed separately.
Modify WHATABOUT	The WHATABOUT field can be accessed separately.
Store W5 tuple	Tuples can be stored in this sub-system.
Persist	Tuples can be permanently stored.
Save transiently	Tuples can be transiently saved in memory.

Table 3.9: Data Model Layer: Detailed Use Case Description

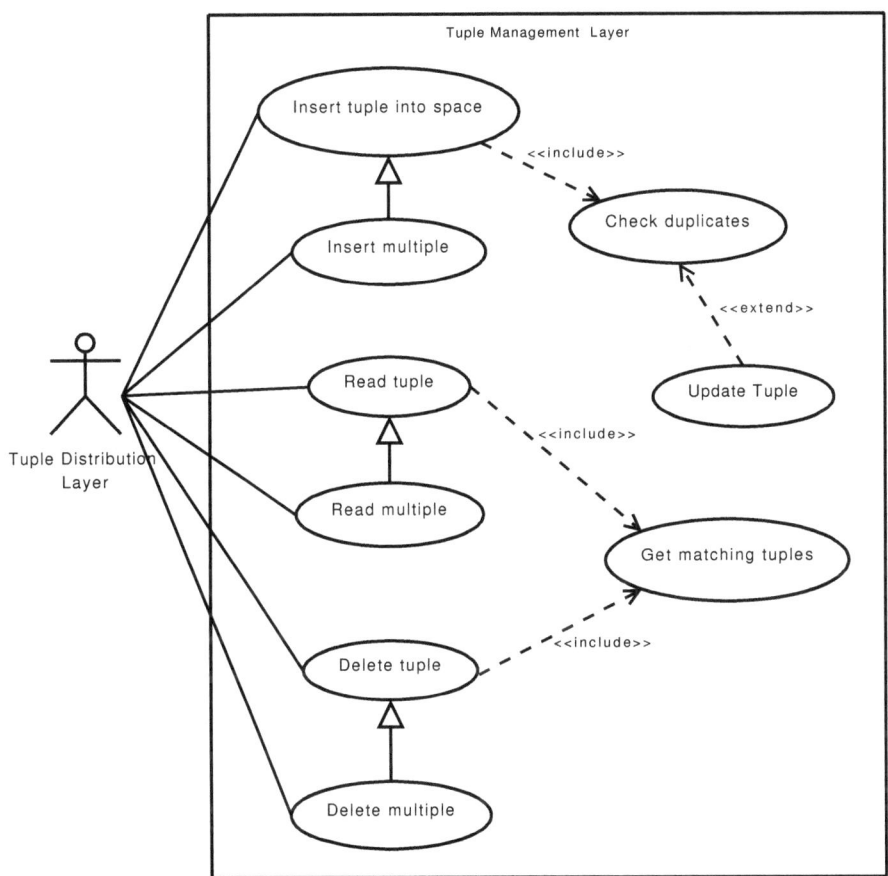

Figure 3.28: Tuple Management Layer: Use Case Diagram

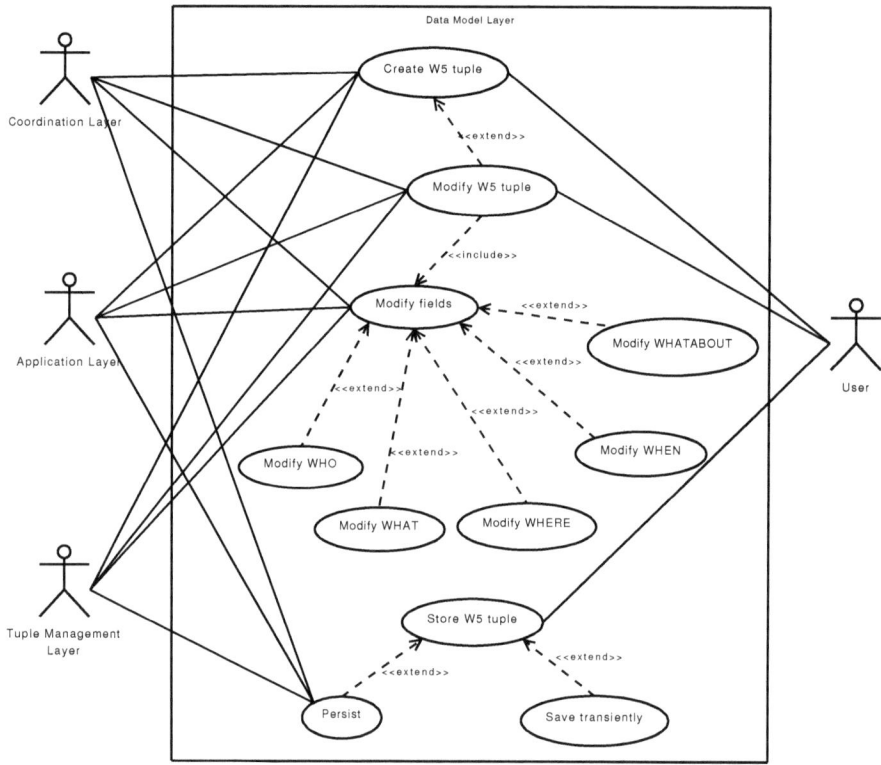

Figure 3.29: Data Model Layer: Use Case Diagram

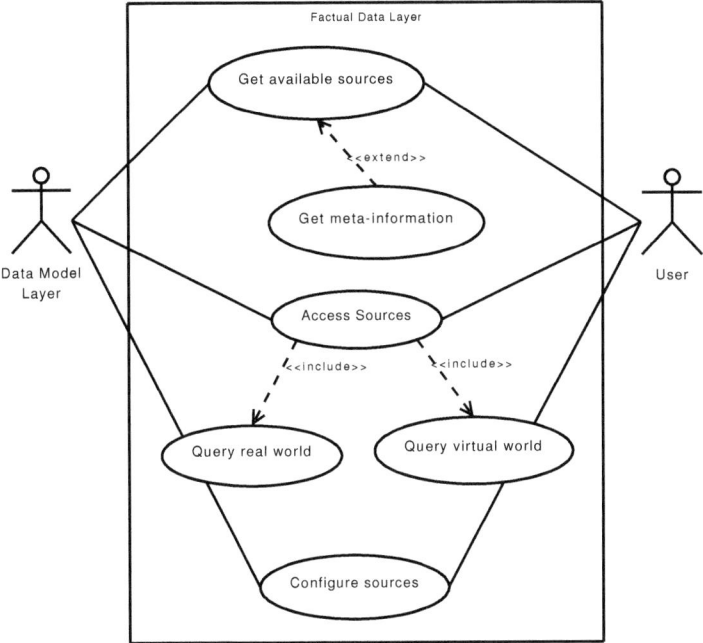

Figure 3.30: Factual Data Layer: Use Case Diagram

Factual Data Layer Use Cases

The actors of this sub-system are the user and the data model sub-system. Figure 3.30 and Table 3.10 provide the necessary details.

3.3.2 Components and Classes

This Section provides the detailed software design of the CorA prototypical implementation. For this, UML component and class diagrams are presented and discussed. Also, the relation to the LighTS[29] open-source framework is shown. LighTS is the basis for the fundamental space operations in CorA but has been extensively adapted by sub-classing the relevant classes. This was necessary as CorA aims at portable devices and for this exploits a Virtual Machine of Java 2 Micro Edition (J2ME). LighTS does not fully support this. During the design of CorA much attention was paid to extensibility and re-usability. For this, software design patterns as proposed in [67] where deployed whenever possible. This deployment—where appropriate—is highlighted in the

---

[29]See http://lights.sourceforge.net

Use Case	Description
Get available sources	Actors can retrieve information about available sources.
Get meta-information	Actors can retrieve meta-information about such sources.
Access Sources	Actors can access the sources.
Query real world	The access to sources includes the possibility to query the "real" world.
Query virtual world	The "virtual" world can be queried (e.g. web-based resources), too.
Configure sources	Actors can configure and manage sources.

Table 3.10: Factual Data Layer: Detailed Use Case Description

subsequent Subsections.

Figure 3.31 depicts an overview about how the main packages and components are structured and shows the interfaces among them. CorA subsumes four main packages:

1. The tuple space package (contains the other three packages and the tuple space component)

2. The pattern package (contains the five patterns introduced by CorA (see also Section 3.2.1.5): supervisor/worker, location-oriented coordination, meeting, blackboard, and negotiating)

3. The replication package (contains the replication and communication component)

4. The model package (contains W5 model and the serialization component)

The tuple space package provides interfaces to external applications as depicted in Figure 3.31. All of these four packages are introduced in more detail in the following Subsections.

Tuple Space Package

The classes and their structure are depicted in Figure 3.32. The main control class is the tuple space management **TSManager** which is implemented as a Singleton pattern. Via the **ITupleListener** interface a **TupleChangedEvent** can be registered in the **TSManager**. Whenever a relevant tuple is changed this event fires. More details on the internal logics are provided in Section 3.3.3. In order to create **W5TupleSpace** objects the **W5TupleSpaceFactory** is needed which is implemented as an Abstract Factory pattern. The **W5TupleSpace** class and the **IW5TupleSpace** are derived from corresponding entities of the LighTS framework.

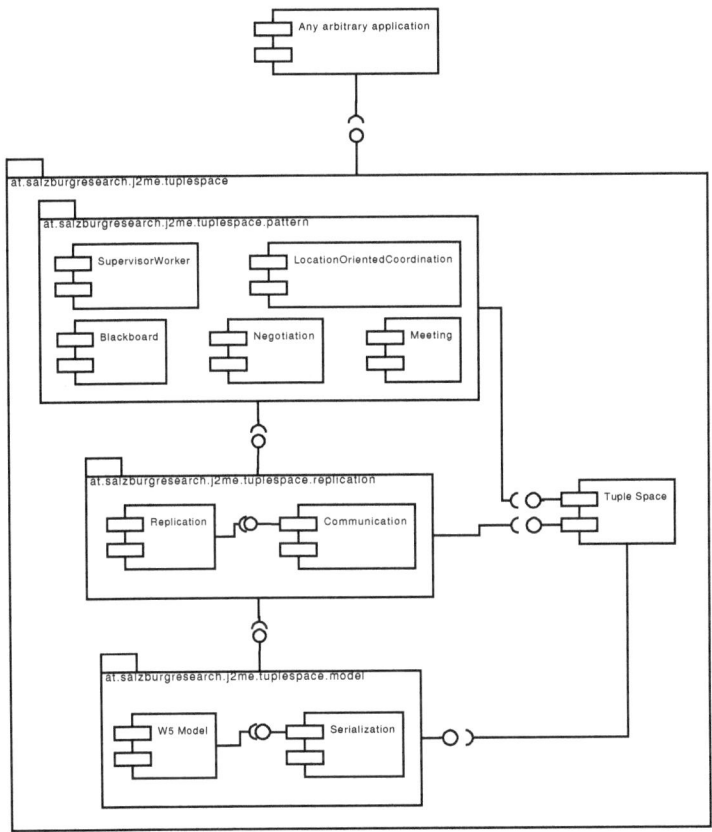

Figure 3.31: CorA Component Diagram

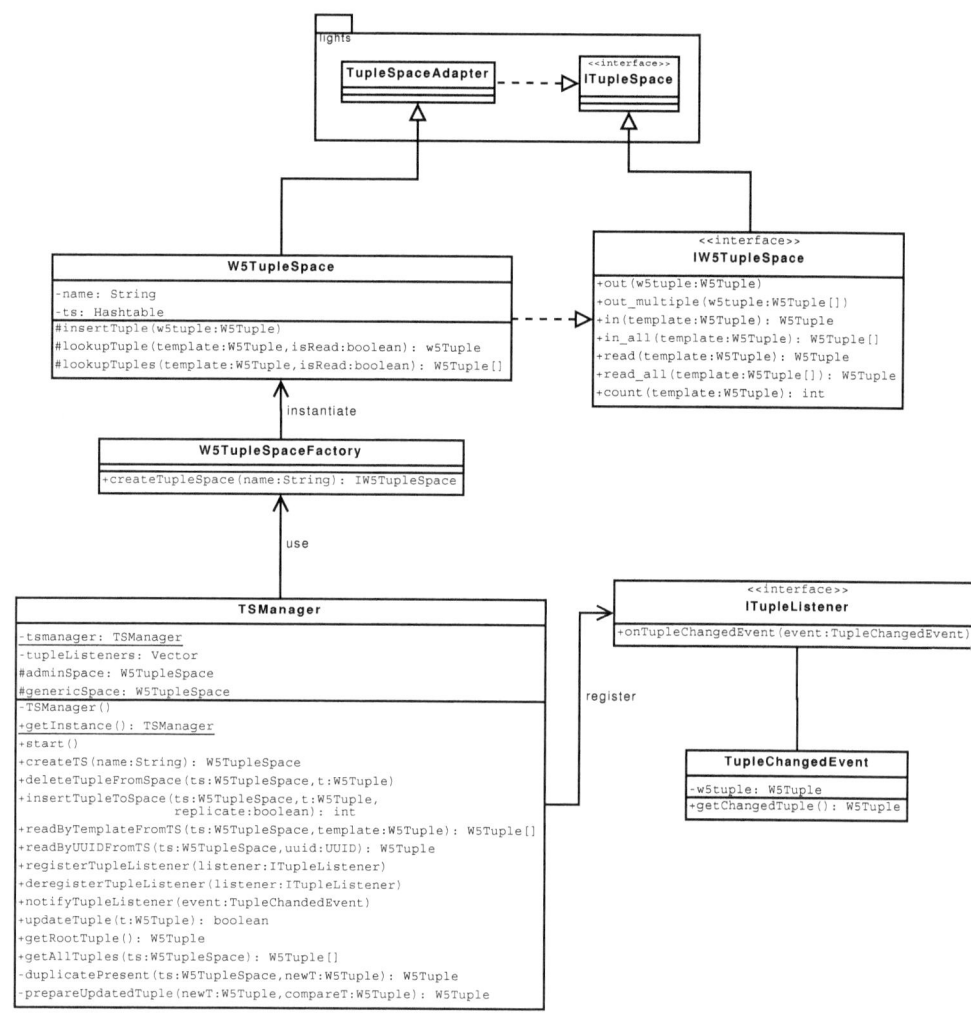

Figure 3.32: Class Diagram of the Tuple Space Package

Pattern Package

The patterns introduced in the concept of the coordination architecture were described and illustrated earlier (Section 3.2.1.5). The corresponding class diagrams in Section 3.2.1.5 of the supervisor/worker pattern (see Figure 3.10 on page 42), the location-oriented coordination pattern (see Figure 3.11 on page 44), the meeting pattern (see Figure 3.12 on page 46), the blackboard pattern (see Figure 3.13 on page 47), and the negotiating pattern (see Figure 3.14 on page 48) are depicted in a generalized way. The differences to the concrete reference implementation of CorA presented here are only marginal—such as the modelling of the entities as W5 tuples. Hence, this is not repeated here but we refer to these earlier sections.

Replication Package

The replication package deals with two basic issues (both shown in Figure 3.33): *(i)* replicating the tuples between the peers and *(ii)* establishing communication between the peers in order to be able to replicate. The replication component is implemented as a Strategy design pattern. The various strategies were introduced and formalized in Section 3.2.2. This Section shows only the embodiment in the concrete CorA framework. Replication strategies can be arbitrarily added. Four strategies are defined in CorA which are represented be according classes: `StrategyFULL_PUSH`, `StrategyFULL_PULL`, `StrategyCONTEXT_PUSH`, and `StrategyCONTEXT_PULL`.

The communication between peers is locally managed by the Singleton `PeerManager`, which deals with addresses of peers (kept by a dedicated W5TupleSpace responsible for administrative data and managed by the class `TSManager`) and the communication protocol. Actual sending and receiving of messages is handled by the classes `CommunicationService` and `MessageConnection`. Both are kept flexible and extensible in terms of concrete transmission technology and protocol deployed. In the current reference implementation of CorA TCP/IP over WLAN is deployed.

The type of communication between peers is handled by a construct complying with the Chain-of-Responsibility (more accurately Tree-of-Responsibility) design pattern. According to different codes (representing the various types of communication) encapsulated in messages, these are treated differently, which leads to a higher modularity of the software design. Figure 3.33 lists these different codes (see the abstract class `CommunicationProtocolHandler`).

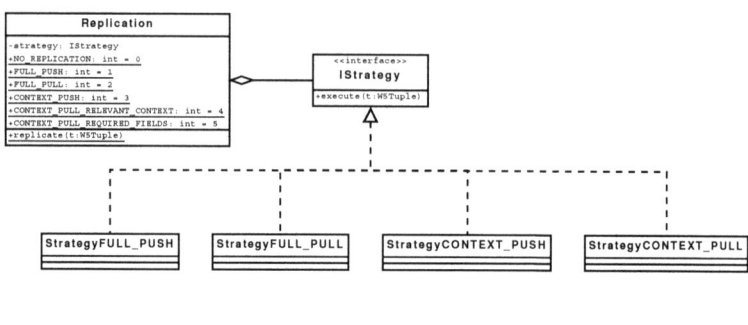

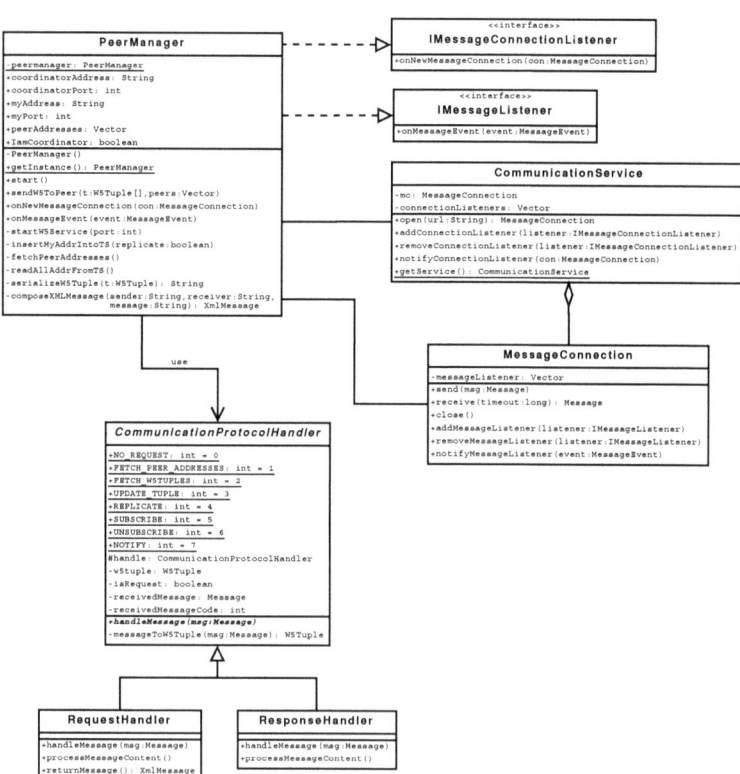

Figure 3.33: Class Diagram of the Replication Package

Model Package

The model package essentially represents the implementation of the W5 concept in terms of an object-oriented approach which makes heavy usage of delegation, composition, and aggregation concepts. The W5 structure with its five facts *Who*, *What*, *Where*, *When*, and *Whatabout* was introduced in Section 3.2.1.2 and is not repeated here. Each such fact type is represented by an according class (see Figure 3.35) and are composed together by the `W5Tuple` class, which in turn is derived from a related class within LighTS.

To some extent, replication is also addressed in the model package. Each tuple itself carries the information about how it needs to be replicated. The replication logic is encapsulated in the replication package. This is stored in the meta-information fact (*Whatabout*) of any W5 tuple. The following fields are covered by *Whatabout*:

timestamp: long	Creation of the object.
belongsToSpace: String	Membership to a particular space.
keepOldTuple: boolean	Updated tuples are kept in space for a history.
updateTuple: boolean	The tuple must not be updated.
readOnly: boolean	The tuple is for reading only.
localOnly: boolean	The tuple exists only locally.
persistTuple: boolean	The tuple must be persisted.
replStrat: int	Defines the replication strategy to be used.
protocol: int	Defines the communication protocol.
versionvector: Hashtable	Keeps the updates in a version vector.
peerAddr: String	The URL of the current peer.

The whole construct is extensible in an arbitrary manner. The reference implementation already provides classes representing particular payload information such as `DescriptionPayload`, `MapPayload`, `PointPayload`, `PolylinePayload`, and `TimeFactPayload` all derived from the abstract `Payload` class. A lot of necessary information can already be modelled with this set of payload objects.

Due to the fact, that serialization is not supported per se in J2ME and CorA primarily aims at J2ME enabled handheld devices, we devised and implemented a serialization framework, with which we are able to serialize and de-serialize `W5Tuple` objects prior to sending it over a network or prior to persisting. The framework covers all payload objects defined so far. The structure is depicted in Figure 3.35.

More details about internal logics (in particular about the tuple update process and the related structure and examination of the version vector) and about how to use the CorA API are presented in subsequent chapters.

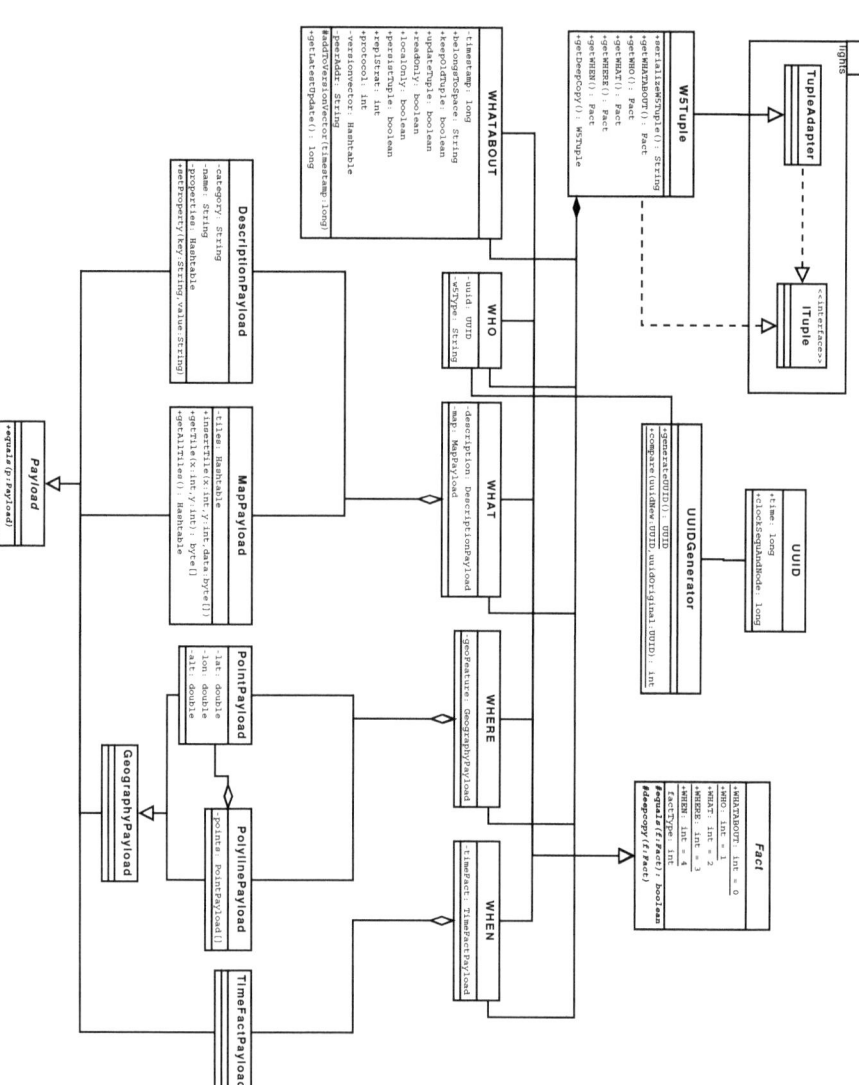

Figure 3.34: Class Diagram of the Model Package

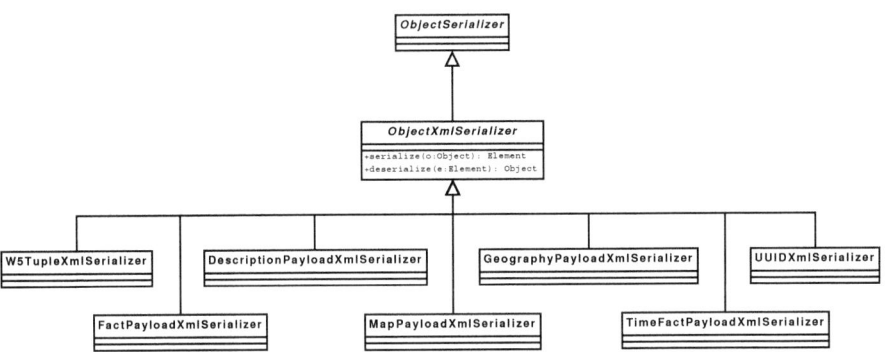

Figure 3.35: Class Diagram of the Serialization Package

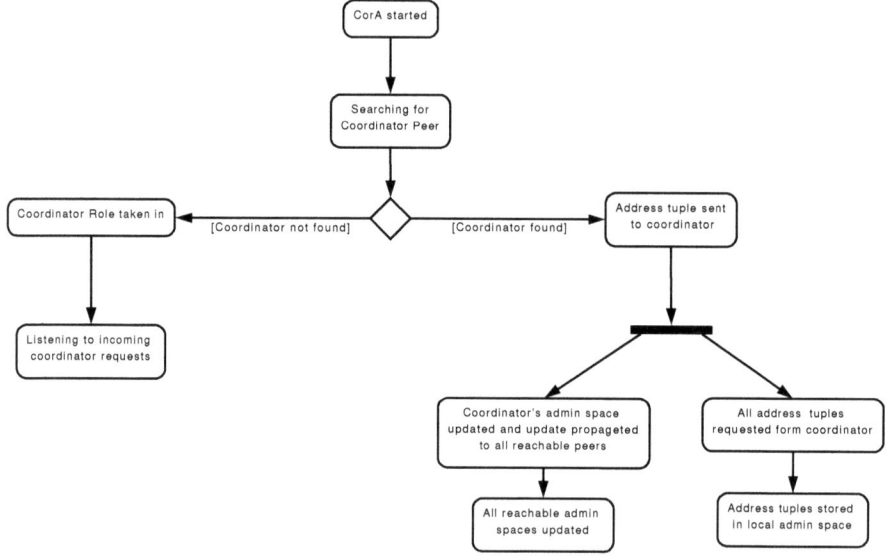

Figure 3.36: Basic States during the Start-up of CorA

3.3.3 CorA's Internal Logics

This section presents some relevant internal or business logics of CorA. These logics are:

- The start-up process
- The registration of the peer address
- The tuple update process
- The Inspection of duplicate tuples
- The Examination of the version vector

Figure 3.36 essentially depicts the states during start-up of a CorA peer. A peer tries to find a peer exhibiting the coordinator role. If none can be detected, the peer itself takes on this role. If one can be found the peer transmits his peer address (i.e. URL) and asks to get the URLs of all the other peers currently in reach.

The sequence diagram of Figure 3.37 gives more details about the internal actions when a peer transmits its URL and needs to fetch all available other peer addresses during start-up. After the coordinator has received the address information of the sending peer and after storing this new address tuple in the tuple space, this information is replicated according to the defined replication strategy to all other reachable peers. By default, in this case the replication strategy is the FULL_PUSH strategy.

The sequence diagram in Figure 3.38 depicts an overview about how a tuple is received by a peer and then stored to the tuple space. The TSManager performs two important operations in order to make sure that storing this tuple to the space is correct: duplicatePresent() and prepareUpdatedTuple().

A tuple, however, can also be locally updated, hence, it is not necessary that a tuple is coming from the network.

First, Figure 3.39 illustrates the activities necessary for checking if there is already a duplicate tuple present in the space.

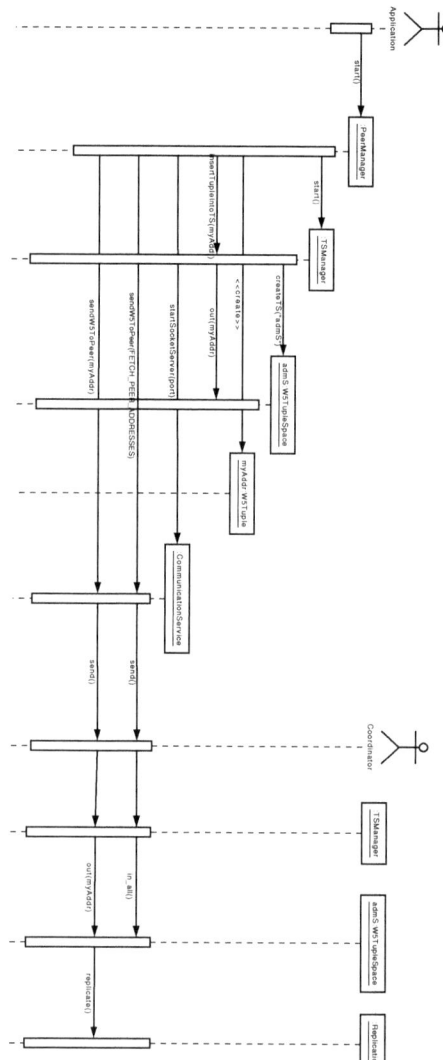

Figure 3.37: The Peer Registration Process

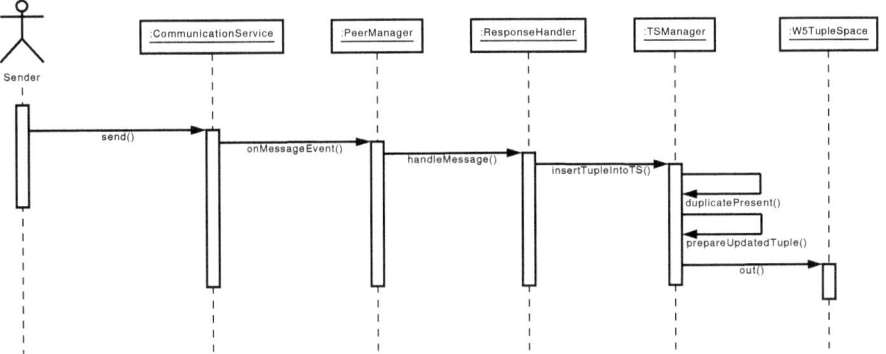

Figure 3.38: The Sequence of a Tuple Update

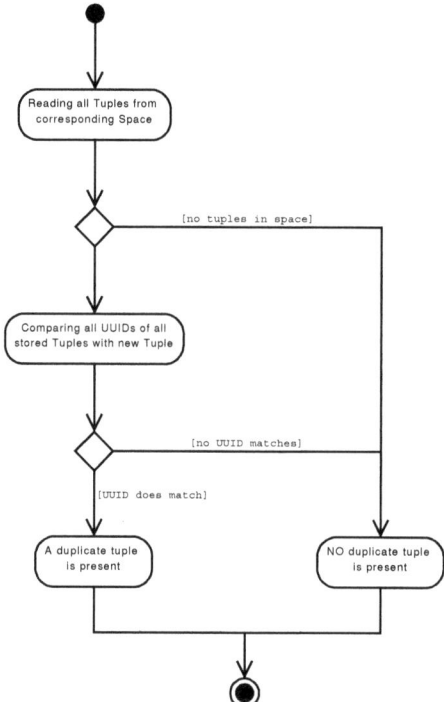

Figure 3.39: Inspecting Present Tuple Duplicates

Second, the `TSManager` inspects which of the tuples is more up-to-date or which fields need to be updated and how the tuple has to be processed further–in terms of how to replicate and whether the outdated tuple needs to be kept in the space.

The method `prepareUpdatedTuple()` has two arguments, namely the new `W5Tuple` called `newT` and the duplicate one already stored in the space `compareT`. It returns the one `W5Tuple` which finally must be stored in the space. In order to determine the right tuple the concept of the version vectors as introduced in Section 3.2.1.4 is exploited. In CorA, the version vector is implemented as a `Hashtable` object that keeps the addresses of the peers (i.e. URLs) as keys. The corresponding values are kept as `Vector` objects which in turn keep timestamps as `Long` objects indicating when the tuple has been modified.

Figure 3.40 illustrates the basic activities conducted in the `prepareUpdatedTuple()` method.

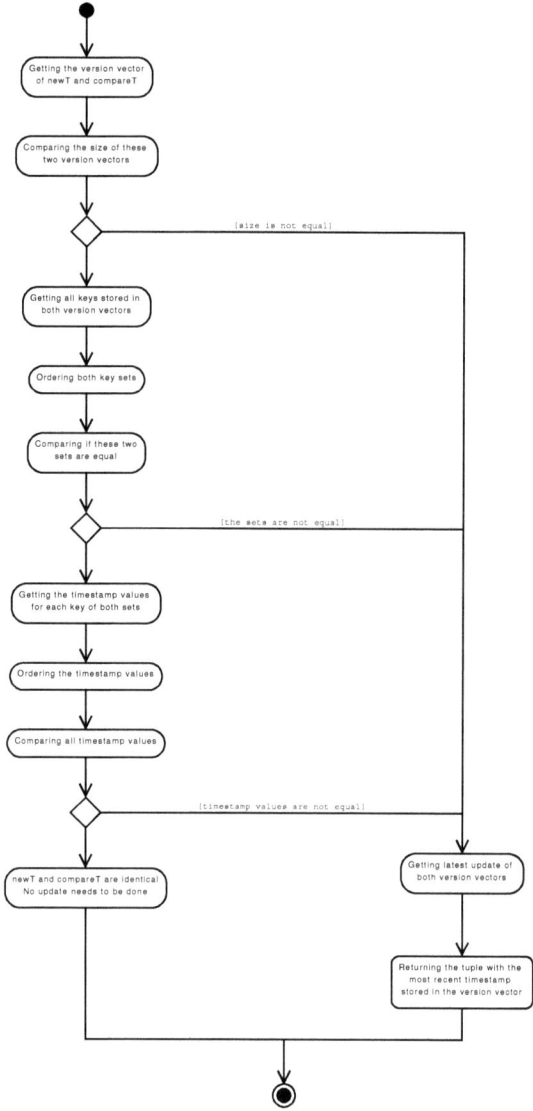

Figure 3.40: Preparing Tuple for Subsequent Update in Space

3.3.4 Application Programming Interface

This section provides an excerpt of the most essential API usages for application programmers. The most important methods provided by the CorA middleware are introduced.

The `PeerManager` class is a Singleton and deals with the basic operations necessary to manage the connectivity with other peers in the network.

    PeerManager pm = PeerManager.getInstance();

the reference to the one Singleton instance of the `PeerManager` is stored into `pm`.

    pm.setCoordinatorAddress(String coordinatorAddress);

tells the `PeerManager` the well-known URL to the coordinator peer. In the current implementation of CorA this information is stored in the Midlet JAD (Java Application Descriptor) as a property. This JAD property can be retrieved by the `getAppProperty` method of the J2ME `MIDlet` class.

    pm.setURL(String protocol, String IPAddress, int port);

sets the URL of the peer, where in CorA the IP and the port initially are also retrieved from the JAD.

    pm.peerIsCoordinator();

is used to check if the peer is already in the coordinator peer role, if a coordinator is available, or if the peer needs to take in the coordinator role (see also Figure 3.36).

    pm.start();

finally causes the `PeerManager` to start operating and interacting with other peers and the local tuple spaces.

The `TSManager` class is also a Singleton and deals with the basic operations necessary to manage the local spaces and also to initiate necessary replication mechanisms which, in turn, are then propagated and managed via the internal logics of the `PeerManager`.

Two further essential classes relevant for interacting with the CorA middleware are the class `W5Tuple` implementing the tuple concept introduced in Section 3.2.1.2 (see also Figure 3.34 for the class diagram) and the class `W5TupleSpace` implementing the local tuple spaces (see also Figure 3.32 for the class diagram).

An example using and modifying a `PointPayload` object inside a `W5Tuple` object should help to explain this API.

```
PointPayload pp = new PointPayload(
        long lat, long lon, long alt);
```

the new object `pp` is constructed with three arguments of type `long`.

```
W5Tuple w5 = new W5Tuple(
        PeerManager.getInstance().getMyAddress());
```

a new `W5Tuple` object is created. The constructor needs the address of the current peer as argument (This is necessary for the version vectors).

```
w5.where.setGeoFeature(PointPayload pp);
```

any object of type `W5Tuple` has five aggregated objects `who`, `what`, `where`, `when`, and `whatabout`. As shown in this example `where` is responsible for locations. Hence, the `pp` object can be assigned.

```
w5.what.getDescription().setCategory(String category);
```

a catalogue of freely selectable category names can be chosen. Each tuple can be assigned to one of these categories. An appropriate category name for our tuple object would be "position". Such a category is encapsulated in the `what` object and further in the `DescriptionPayload` object.

```
w5.whatabout.keepOldTuple = true;
```

means that whenever a newer version of the tuple w5 is inserted into the space the old one is still kept in the space in order to have a stored history of changed tuples.

```
w5.whatabout.replStrat = Replication.FULL_PUSH;
```

by this the strategy about how to replicate a tuple can be defined. The class `Replication` defines five basic replication strategies as integer constants: NO_REPLICATION, FULL_PUSH, FULL_PULL, CONTEXT_PUSH, or CONTEXT_PULL.

```
UUID uuid = w5.who.getUUID();
```

the UUID of the `w5` object can be retrieved for later reference.

```
TSManager tsm = TSManager.getInstance();
```

the reference to the one Singleton instance of the `TSManager` is stored into `tsm`.

```
tsm.start()
```

the necessary preconditions for the tuple space operations—such as creating the necessary space instances—are triggered.

```
tsm.insertTupleIntoTS(W5TupleSpace ts, W5Tuple w,
        boolean replicate);
```

this method encapsulates the insertion (and update if necessary) of a tuple `w` into the space `ts`. If `replicate` is `true` then this tuple is also replicated according to the strategy defined in `w`.

```
W5Tuple w5tuple = tsm.getTuple(UUID uuid);
```

a tuple can be read from the tuple space by providing the UUID as argument if known.

```
W5Tuple[] results = tsm.getByTemplate(w5);
```

if UUIDs are not known tuples can also be read by providing a template. In this case the template is the w5 tuple that was created earlier. This way the structure of the `W5Tuple` objects are compared and returned if they match the structure of the template. All matching tuples are copied (i.e. deep copy) into a `W5Tuple` array.

The following code snippets show how to alter a tuple after retrieval and subsequent re-injection into the space.

```
w5tuple.where.setGeoFeature(new PointPayload(
        newLat, newLon, newAlt));
```

sets three new `long` values into the `PointPayload` object of the `where` field of the `w5tuple` we earlier retrieved from the space.

```
tsm.insertTupleIntoTS(tsm.genS, w5tuple, true);
```

the `w5tuple` is inserted into the generic space. The `TSManager` instance `tsm` holds at least two `W5TupleSpace` instances, namely `admS` for administrative tuples and `genS` for operative tuples which is the default tuple space. This change needs to be replicated to all other peers (indicated by `true` as the last argument).

3.4 Chapter Summary

In this Chapter we presented one particular field where the optimisation potential of improved coordination can be exploited, which is harnessing coordination for collaboration. First, we gave an introduction to the area of Computer Supported Cooperative Work (CSCW). We conducted a word by word analysis of each term in CSCW. We also introduced a taxonomy for CSCW applications according to space and time. The most relevant applications are those that are asynchronous in time, spatially distributed, and involve mobile users. The research discipline that is concerned with this type of mobile collaboration is referred to as Telecooperation, to which we also classify our research.

Second, we stated that we particularly focus on mobile collaboration, which is defined as mobile users who are working together to achieve a common goal. Mobile collaboration scenarios can be supported by pervasive information systems. Hence, these are embedded in pervasive environments. We discussed the evolution of information systems beginning from Vannevar Bush's vision about the Memex and continuing with Mark Weiser's vision about ubiquitous computing systems and the Internet of Things. We gave several definitions of pervasive computing and defined the notion that we use throughout this book. With respect to engineering of applications for pervasive environments we introduced two important principles, namely the Boundary and the Volatility Principles. We also discussed several challenges and how they could be addressed such as different programming and middleware paradigms, adaptation and related it to context-awareness, and several others such as hardware and sensors, human-computer interaction, security and privacy, or self-organization.

As one representative example for mobile collaboration we introduced emergency management. Emergency management serves as the application example where CorA is deployed in various ways, which is shown and evaluated later in the book.

We continued by presenting the design of the conceptual coordination architecture CorA. The design decisions were based on a requirements analysis where several well-known and established pervasive scenarios from different sources were investigated. In order to clearly separate the various concerns, CorA is designed as a layered architecture comprising the following six layers: factual data layer, data model layer, tuple management layer, tuple distribution layer, coordination layer, and application layer. One design goal was to architecturally address the challenge of pervasive computing of matching the physical world with the virtual world. For this, the factual data layer considers various different data sources which can be integrated on the higher data model layer. The data model layer, essentially, encapsulates the W5 data model that is capable of processing context along four dimensions (*Who, What, Where, When*) and additionally provides self-description of tuples by the *Whatabout* field. For communication and information distribution in the mobile P2P network of CorA we designed a distributed tuple space based system with various replication strategies. Replication is a core functionality of CorA. Devising and reasoning about the four strategies was accomplished by the help of the Mobile UNITY formalism. formalizing and system engineering altered and was conducted in parallel. Finally, the coordination laws (i.e., the mechanisms to resolve interdependencies) are encapsulated in CorA's coordination layer. Mainly, relevant mechanisms are abstracted to coordination patterns that help to tackle well-known coordination problems by proposing appropriate solutions. The coordination patterns catalogue contains the following patterns: supervisor/worker pattern, location-oriented coordination pattern, meeting pattern, blackboard pattern, and negotiating pattern.

Finally, the Chapter gave implementation details about the coordination language. It covered the system use cases addressed by each architectural layer of CorA. Details about the software system design on the level of components and classes were presented, which implied the four main packages: the tuple space, the pattern, the replication, and the model package. Several UML Sequence Diagrams illustrated essential internal and business logics of CorA, such as the start-up process, the registration of the peer address, the tuple update process, the inspection of duplicate tuples, and the examination of the version vector which is mainly required for replication and updates. Finally, the usage of the CorA middleware application programming interface (API) was explained.

After having presented the concept behind CorA and the concrete implementation, the next Chapter gives details about the various tests and applications conducted for the subsequent evaluation of the approach of this book.

Chapter 4

Evaluation of the Optimisation Potential in Collaboration

This Chapter evaluates how the presented approach can address the optimisation potential offered through improved coordination in the application area of collaboration. We describe the experiments conducted and the application of CorA to a mobile collaboration example from emergency management. The analysis is threefold. First, on a *system-level* tests are performed in order to quantitatively measure the CorA system behaviour. Second, the concept and implementation of CorA are applied to the works conducted during the European research Project WORKPAD. We qualitatively evaluate the provision and integration (through well-defined APIs) of CorA into a larger pervasive information system for mobile collaboration on a *developer-level*. Third, we conduct user validations in order to get feedback on a *user-level*.

In this Chapter we additionally give information about related areas and place it in the context of the approach presented in this book. Finally, the approach of this work together with the results of various tests and the application is interpreted and a critical reflection is given.

4.1 Evaluation on System-Level

This Section summarizes the system tests which serve as the basis for the evaluation of the performance of the coordination architecture CorA and its reference implementation as introduced in Sections 3.2 and 3.3, respectively. For this, the following Section 4.1.1 describes what is tested and why, Subsection 4.1.2 gives details about the test set-up with respect to hardware and software, and Subsection 4.1.3 finally presents the test results.

4.1.1 Test Strategy

In order to develop a system that does support collaborative work in pervasive environments certain system behaviours must be respected during development. Two essential criteria [89, 166] of distributed systems that embody metrics to measure such behaviour are: *(i) scalability*, and *(ii) consistency*.

Scalability is the characteristic of a system describing that the addition or subtraction of resources does not noticeably influence its performance [125]. The degree of that influence is very much depending on the type and size of a distributed system and the required applications.

Consistency [89] describes the internal state of various entities within a distributed system. In a 100% consistent system all entities have equal internal states during all times. Also, the degree of consistency depends on the same circumstances as scalability.

Both are naturally interdependent. In order to reach a consistent state, the entities in a system must communicate their state to others and agree upon a common one. Scalable communication protocols must ensure that a consistent state can be reached. Consistency, however, must not be reached at all costs. It is counterproductive to affect the system behaviour negatively (e.g. its scalability) due to a strict consistency policy. Hence, a trade-off between scalability and consistency needs to be defined for a distributed system.

Scalability and consistency—as the two investigated criteria—are tightly coupled to the information distribution techniques and algorithms embodied in the replication mechanisms provided by CorA. Hence, by focusing on these two conclusions shall be drawn about the applicability of CorA with respect to the defined mobile collaboration domain.

4.1.2 Test Set-up

In order to test scalability and consistency of CorA's distributed tuple space architecture and the replication mechanisms, several test-runs with several peers and different traffic (i.e., tuple) generators are executed. Several tuple generators were developed that randomly interact with the local tuple space by creating, modifying or deleting tuples. The replication mechanisms in the CorA middleware have to propagate these changes to all other involved peers. The tuple generators are implemented according to the Strategy Design Pattern [67]. In order to simulate a realistic scenario and to produce realistic traffic four different types of generators were developed:

1. `PeriodicGenerator`: a new tuple is created and inserted into the tuple space according to a freely definable time period in seconds.

2. `RandomGenerator`: a new tuple is created and inserted into the tuple space with a random time interval in seconds between each creation. The upper and lower bound of this interval can be defined.

3. `OverwriteGenerator`: a tuple is created once and inserted into the tuple space. According to a freely definable time period in seconds this tuple is taken out of the space, its contained data is modified, and inserted into the space again.

PeerID	PeriodicGenerator	RandomGenerator	OverwriteGenerator	RemoveGenerator
P0	X			
P1			X	
P2		X		
P3		X		X
P4	X			

Table 4.1: Test Case 1: Generator Configuration

4. `RemoveGenerator`: a random tuple is deleted from the tuple space. This happens after a random time interval in seconds where the upper and lower bound can be freely configured.

The local spaces at each peer are constantly monitored and each change is logged in a local file together with a timestamp and relevant contents of the various tuples. For each space deployed on each peer one file is generated. The files are analysed after the test runs (see Section 4.1.3).

As also indicated in Section 3.3.4, the CorA reference implementation of the tuple space middleware foresees at least two types of local tuple spaces (i.e., the `W5TupleSpace`): namely, the *admin space* for administrative tuples (such as address information) and the *generic space* for operative tuples which is the default tuple space. It is important to mention that the main subject of investigation of the test cases presented in this Section is the generic space as this is the space that is accessed by much more operations. In contrast, the admin space is rather static. As soon as all the address information (during start-up time) is distributed there is hardly any change. This is also due to the rather static set-up where we emulate all the peers on one computer. As both spaces are equally implemented the behaviour is expected to be entirely equal. Hence, it is correct to closely investigate the generic space and from the results to generalize the behaviour of all instances of `W5TupleSpaces`.

Basically, we defined two test cases: the first case subsumes a configuration of five peers, the second ten peers. Each test is executed for ten minutes during which about 8000 tuples are created and stored in each generic space per peer. We take probes every 30 seconds. This is done in order to check the current local state and compare with other spaces for deducing the behaviour regarding consistency.

Furthermore, we measure the time span around each probe until a consistent state is reached over all involved peers. This is directly related to the scalability criterion. Also, scalability is investigated by comparing the behaviour of the first test case (five peers) with the second (ten peers).

Table 4.1 depicts the configuration of peers and the deployed types of generators for the first test case; Table 4.2 for the second case.

After some preliminary test runs, adequate values for the periods and upper and lower bounds for random calculations evolved which are used for all test runs. These values summarized in Table 4.3.

Each test case was additionally conducted twice in order to diminish potential effects that may be caused by the (pseudo-)random algorithms deployed for tuple generations.

PeerID	PeriodicGenerator	RandomGenerator	OverwriteGenerator	RemoveGenerator
P0	X			
P1			X	
P2		X		
P3		X		X
P4	X			
P5	X			
P6			X	
P7		X		
P8		X		X
P9		X		

Table 4.2: Test Case 2: Generator Configuration

Generator Type	Values
`PeriodicGenerator`	Period=35 seconds
`RandomGenerator`	Random: lower bound=7 seconds, upper bound=55 seconds
`OverwriteGenerator`	Period=35 seconds
`RemoveGenerator`	Random: lower bound=1 second, upper bound=20 seconds

Table 4.3: Time Intervals of Generators

The following hard- and software was used for the test:

Hardware: Lenovo Thinkpad X60 TabletPC (Processor: Intel Core Duo L2400 / 1.67 GHz, RAM: 1 GB (DDR2 SDRAM), Cache: 2 MB (L2 cache), Hard Drive: 60 GB, Wireless capabilities: 802.11a,b,g and Bluetooth)

Software: Eclipse (version 3.2.2), EclipseME (version 1.6.5), Sun Java VM (version 1.6.0_03), Sun Wireless Toolkit (version 2.5.2)

4.1.3 Test Results

Taking into account the production of about 8000 tuples per space per peer (only in the generic space) as mentioned earlier (Section 4.1.2), a total of 240000 tuples[1] were processed during the experimental system tests. This Section prepares the test results[2] extracted from this amount of data.

At specifically defined points in time all spaces of the peers need to be equal (means equal amount of tuples and equal tuples). The duration of each test run was ten minutes (=600 seconds). A snapshot of the generic space was taken every 30 seconds which results in 20 probes per test run. For each of these probes, we counted the number of equal tuples in the space over all peers at a time, calculated the mean and the standard deviation.

Additionally, we determined the average time span of this deviation (i.e., how long it takes on average until a consistent state between all local generic spaces of all peers is established). For this, we calculate the difference in time regarding the earliest snapshot of a peer i and the latest snapshot of a peer j where the tuples of the snapshot are equal.

---

[1] 8000 tuples per peer x 15 peers (5 peers of the first test case + 10 peers of the second) x 2 (as both cases were executed twice)
[2] The raw data of the results can be obtained by contacting the author.

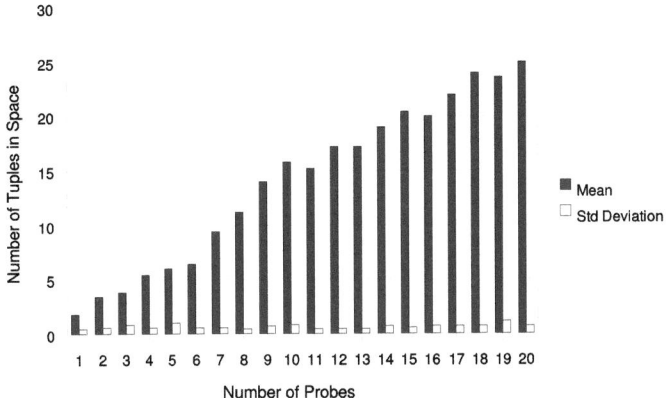

Figure 4.1: Mean and Std Deviation of First Test Case (First Run)

First Test Case Results

The Figures 4.1 and 4.2 depict the results of the probes of the first test case (five peers): Figure 4.1 summarizes the first run and Figure 4.2 the second. The dark bars indicate the average number of tuples in the generic space over the involved peers per probe. The bright bars represent the standard deviations. The behaviour of both runs is very similar. The number of tuples naturally increases over time in a similar pattern. Also the standard deviation is similarly low. In the second test run the deviation is frequently zero. The average standard deviation over all probes of the first run adds up to 0.65. In the second test run it is 0.22.

Figure 4.3 compares the consistency time span—i.e., the time needed for establishing a consistent state—between the two test runs of the first test case. No particular pattern can be recognised. The graphs are non-deterministic. The average consistency time span over all probes is very similar: in the first run it is 3.62s, in the second it is 3.37s.

The first test case was conducted twice in order to diminish some random tuple generator side-effects (see Section 4.1.2). The results of both test runs of test case one are indeed different but nevertheless similar. Hence, the random tuple generator effects can be considered as minimal. The aggregated relevant results of both runs add up to a standard deviation of 0.43 and a consistency time span of 3.49s. This results in an average of 0.12 inconsistent tuples per second.

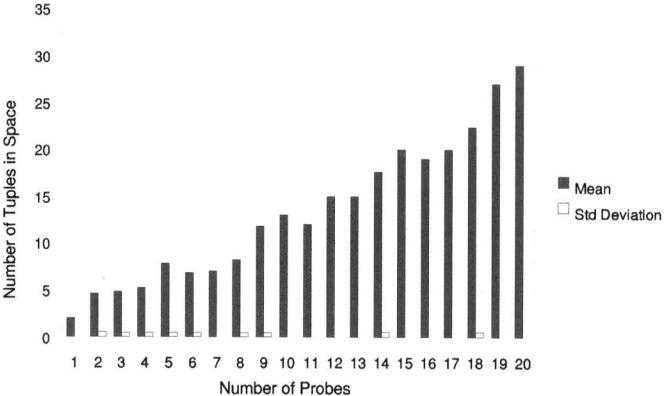

Figure 4.2: Mean and Std Deviation of First Test Case (Second Run)

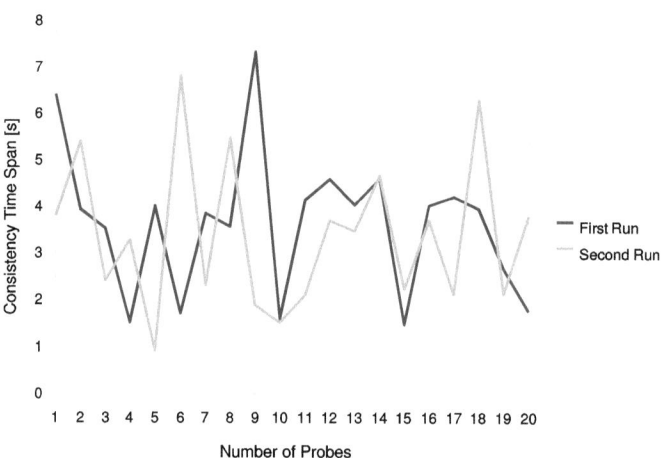

Figure 4.3: Consistency Time Span of First Test Case (First and Second Run)

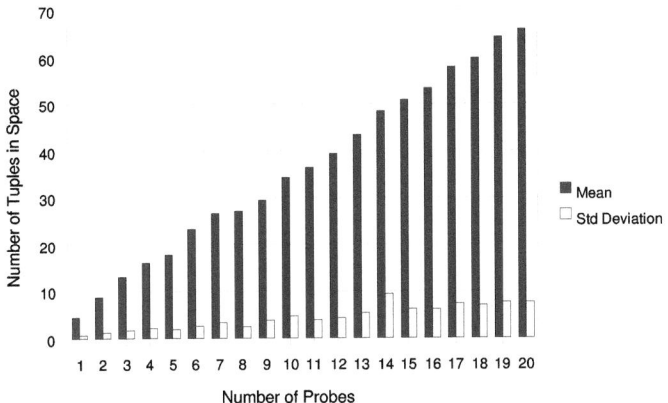

Figure 4.4: Mean and Std Deviation of Second Test Case (First Run)

Second Test Case Results

The Figure 4.4 summarizes the first run of the second test case and Figure 4.5 the second run. Akin to the first test case, the behaviour of both runs in the second case is very similar, too. The standard deviation is slightly increasing towards the end of both test runs. The average standard deviation over all probes of the first run adds up to 4.47. In the second test run it is 4.39.

Figure 4.6 compares the consistency time span between the two test runs of the second test case. Again, no particular pattern or similarity can be recognised. The average consistency time span over all probes is very similar: in the first run it is $8.69s$, in the second it is $8.81s$.

The similarity of the results of both test runs of test case two is even higher than the ones of the first test case. The aggregated relevant results of both runs add up to a standard deviation of 4.43 and a consistency time span of $8.75s$. This results in an average 0.5 inconsistent tuples per second.

Clearly, by comparing the results of the two test cases, the values of the second are higher which corresponds to the higher number of peers involved (first test case: five peers, second test case: ten peers). More peers naturally produce more tuples which results in an exponential increase in traffic and space operations.

For these investigations, only full-push strategy (as presented in detail in Section 3.2.2.2 on page 55 and in Section 3.3 on page 63) is adopted and tested as it is the most "expensive" replication strategy. As we conclude that the consistency and scalability criteria are met for this strategy, these consequently are more than sufficient for all the other strategies.

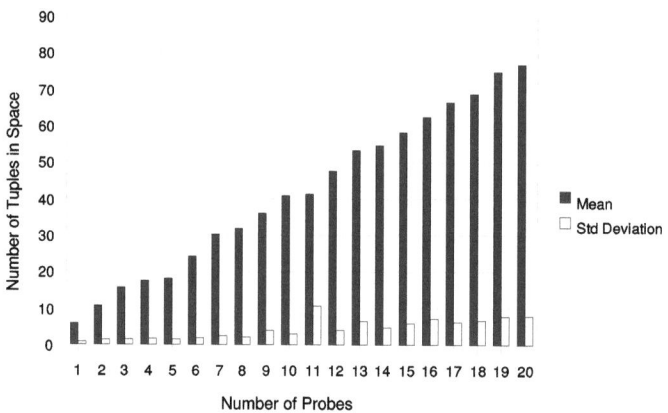

Figure 4.5: Mean and Std Deviation of Second Test Case (Second Run)

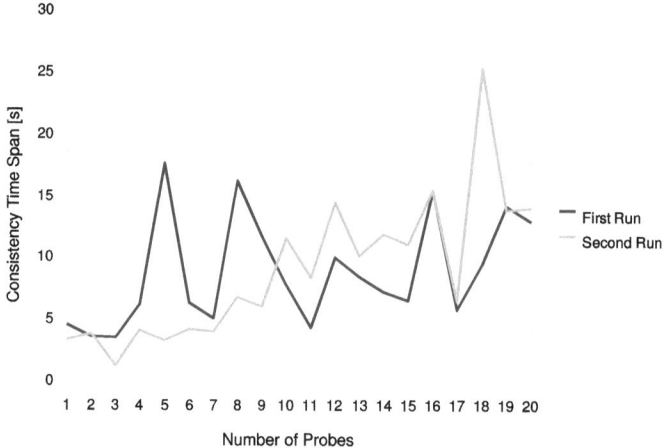

Figure 4.6: Consistency Time Span of Second Test Case (First and Second Run)

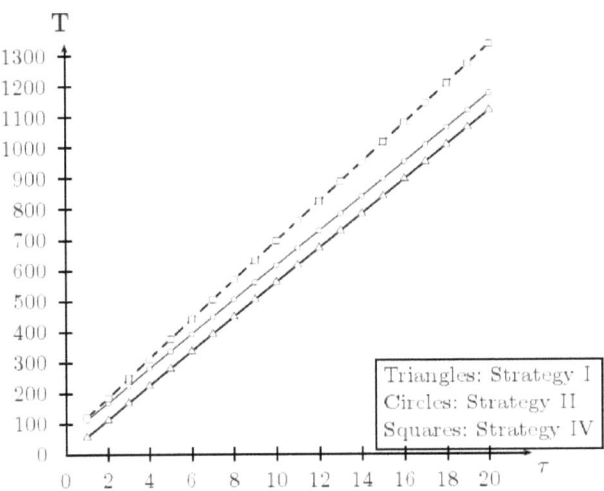

Figure 4.7: Estimation of Replication Costs per Strategy

4.1.4 Replication Cost Analysis

Section 3.2.2 presents details about the replication strategies provided by CorA and for this modells them according to the Mobile UNITY formalism. This Section is only indirectly related to system tests, as the formalization represents the foundation of the replication mechanism implementations. Hence, during the system tests the replication mechanisms are tested implicitly, too. Now, we present some mathematical considerations about the replication costs and the Formulae 3.1, 3.2, 3.3, and 3.4 that were introduced earlier in Section 3.2.2.3 on page 63 for calculating the number of necessary transmissions for each strategy and related to concrete situations.

Figure 4.7 relates the performance of these strategies to each other. The N and N_C, respectively, for this graph are chosen to be 8 participating peers. τ and τ_φ, respectively, are plotted along the horizontal axis. The necessary transmissions T are shown along the vertical axis. In order to make the three graphs comparable the additionally necessary variables for strategy IV are determined to be: N_{Ci} is $N-1$, r_i which is the average number of registrations per peer is one ($r_i = 1$), and E_i which is the average number of firing events per peer is equal to N ($E_i = N$). Strategy number III is not depicted as it is the same graph as for strategy number II.

At a first glance, it could be concluded that strategy number IV is the most costly one. This calculated example, however, is a constructed one. All four strategies very much depend on the situation and the concrete application area. Adopted in the right situation, each strategy clearly has its benefits. Normalized to a common ground—as done by this example shown in Figure 4.7—the context-dependent-push strategy is the most expensive one.

An example highlights the differences: Let the number of participating peers be $N = 8$. Let us assume a scenario in which each peer generates one tuple every ten seconds. After one minute six tuples per peer are available. Hence, let the number of exchanged tuples be $\tau = 6$ in our period under consideration of one minute. The example calculates the following results

$$T_I = 336$$

$$T_{II} = T_{III} = 392$$

$$T_{IV} = 440$$

Still strategy I performs best. However, by introducing a stricter constraint on the context parameter, which is a realistic intervention, influences the context-dependent strategies beneficially. So far, we assumed that all peers are interested in all tuples. This is now cut to half regarding the context-dependent strategies, i.e., by using this type of replication strategy not all tuples are exchanged but only those of interest. For strategies III and IV we assume an average of three tuples per peer to be exchanged ($\tau = 3$). The newly calculated values are

$$T_{III} = 224$$

$$T_{IV} = 80$$

By this exemplified calculation the necessity and advantage of diverse replication strategies become apparent.

4.2 Evaluation on Developer-Level

This Section describes how CorA has been applied to the European research project WORKPAD and the related effects.

4.2.1 Introduction to WORKPAD

WORKPAD (An Adaptive Peer-to-Peer Software Infrastructure for Supporting Cooperative Work of Human Operators in Emergency Scenarios)[3] aims at developing an innovative software infrastructure for supporting collaborative work of human operators in emergency scenarios [84]. In such scenarios, different teams, belonging to different organizations, need to collaborate with each other to reach a common goal. Each team member is equipped with a portable device and carries on specific assigned tasks. In such a way we can consider the whole team as carrying on a process, and different teams collaborate through the interleaving of all the different processes.

The goal is to devise a two-level framework for such scenarios:

1. An integrated back-end (BE) peer-to-peer community, providing advanced services requiring high compu-

---

[3]WORKPAD (FP6-2005-IST-5-034749) is co-funded under the FP6-IST Programme by the European Commission and by the Austrian bm:wf. See http://www.workpad-project.eu

tational power, knowledge and content integration.

2. A set of front-end (FE) peer-to-peer communities, that provide applications, mainly by adaptively enacting processes on mobile ad-hoc networks to human workers.

The FE applications can communicate with the BE and query relevant, potentially integrated, information coming from various content providers.

4.2.2 The WORKPAD System Architecture

From a user's point of view, WORKPAD provides a toolbox containing a set of tools that shall alleviate parts of the work of emergency operators. The operators interact with the tool by using portable devices such as PDAs[4]. The core of WORKPAD is the Adaptive Process Management System that resides on the front-end (FE) and is responsible for coordinating the various tasks representing a process. The Process Management System is tightly connected to the Context Monitoring and Management System. According to changing context information obtained from this system, the Process Management System adaptively changes the process flow. Various user applications are managed by the Process Management and are invoked as necessary and determined by the process. The user interface to the Process Management is the Tasklist Handler that informs the user about tasks that need to be executed. Further applications are the following:

- Multimedia Editor: allows to capture, store, and modify multimedia content.
- Mobile Documentation Tool: allows to electronically document and store various characteristics of a site.
- File Sharing: allows to share any files with other team members on site.
- Mobile Geographic Information System (GIS): allows to interact with geographic information. This tool integrates CorA and is described in detail in Section 4.2.3.

All of these user applications can also directly access the Context Monitoring and Management System if the application needs to exploit context information.

WORKPAD offers also the possibility to retrieve data from a back-end (BE) community of various integrated data sources. Typically, these involve the various data bases of emergency organizations but also external sources that may be of interest such as weather, demographic, or seismic information etc. The FE provides a stub component to which every other FE component can interface to and by this exploit external data coming from the BE. Figure 4.8 illustrates an overview of these main WORKPAD components of the FE.

---

[4]We are aware that in specific cases portable devices are not ideal interfaces in an emergency. In some cases such as during first response phase an extra device may even hamper the operators in accomplishing their tasks. Hence, we regard portable devices as one possible type of interface. Other less obtrusive devices would be wearable interfaces which are still subject to research and not yet mature enough. This, however, is out of scope of the project WORKPAD.

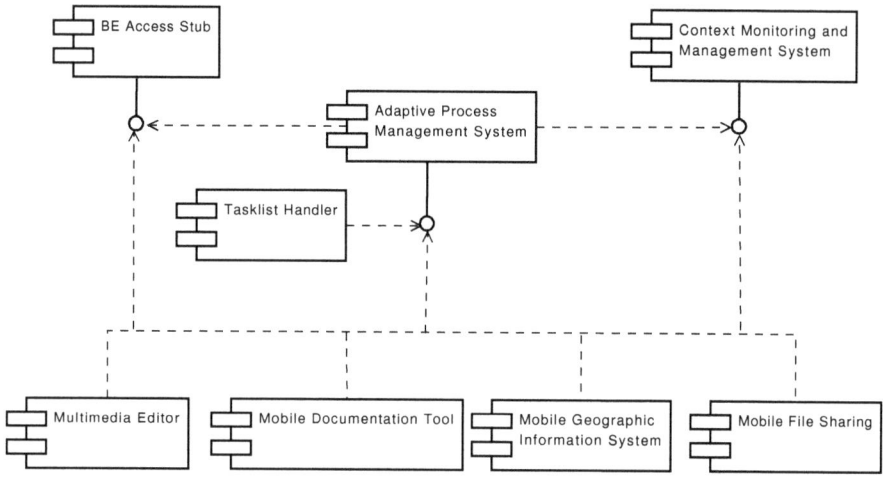

Figure 4.8: Overview of the WORKPAD Components

4.2.3 The Adoption of CorA in WORKPAD

For the WORKPAD project we are developing a mobile geographic information system (GIS) for pervasive environments [15][5]. The coordination architecture CorA is exploited for the realisation of this GIS application. In this Section, we demonstrate the integration of CorA to realise a mobile collaboration application. Moreover, we show an application of the location-oriented coordination pattern to an emergency management (EM) scenario in a pervasive environment. Although EM represents a very well-suited example, we emphasise that the approach presented here could be applied to any collaborative work scenario in pervasive environments where—in this specific case of the LOC pattern—coordination based on spatial objects is relevant. In this Section we describe how CorA and the patterns are integrated and exploited in WORKPAD.

The mobile GIS application is a user application. It provides a graphical user interface allowing the user to interact with the WORKPAD system and its components as outlined in Section 4.2.2. The core functionalities of the mobile GIS application are [16]:

- Presenting geographic information on handheld devices (i.e., enriching ortho-photos with (vector-based) geographic features)

- Browsing geographic information grouped to layers

- Displaying objects- and persons-of-interest (real-time location indication of relevant objects and persons)

- Creating, annotating, and modifying relevant points-of-interest

---
[5]A video demonstrating the main functionalities of this application can be obtained by contacting the author.

- Updating changing geographic information within WORKPAD teams dynamically
- Interacting with the back-end (e.g., querying, persisting)

To realise these functionalities the WORKPAD GIS front-end application internally consists of several components[6]:

1. GIS User Interface Component: handles the rendering of geographic information, the presentation to the user, and provides the appropriate user interfaces (such as PDA interaction per stylus).
2. GIS Middleware: handles the interaction with other WORKPAD components such as the Adaptive Process Management and the Context Monitoring and Management Systems, but also encapsulates the distribution of geographic information to other front-end peers using the mobile GIS application.
3. GIS Back-End Access: handles the access to data stored in the back-end which can either be integrated data from various different sources or geographic data only depending on the information needed by the user.

The second component is the one that deploys CorA and exploits its functionality through API calls. Consequently, all the geographic information is represented according to the W5 model (introduced in Section 3.2.1.2). All the geographic information within the mobile GIS application can be replicated to all involved peers in the front-end. Not all information, however, needs replication. Some is only relevant for the local peer. This can be configured by setting the `localOnly` field in the *Whatabout* fact as described in Section 3.3.2 (page 77). The information that needs replication is replicated as described in Section 3.2.1.4.

Figure 4.9 depicts two screenshots of the mobile GIS application: The part on the left-hand side shows a simple map view with an ortho-photo in the back ground and various geographic features displayed such as areas ("Critical") and points-of-interests ("Field Hospital"). The user can zoom in and out, and rotate and pan the map. By tabbing on "Layers" the user can choose which layers should be displayed on screen. The right-hand part illustrates the context menu that appears when a user tabs the screen with the stylus for a second. The context menu is extensible. In the current version the user can invoke the "Create Annotation" and the "Create Area" functions by this. The created annotation or area is geo-referenced and the information is modelled according to the W5 model and replicated to all the peers of the current configuration.

4.2.4 Exploitation of the GIS Application

In this Section, we show how the mobile GIS application—thus, inherently CorA—is exploited in a showcase event and present the effects on the user (tests on user satisfaction).

---

[6]Only the second component (GIS Middleware), which essentially is CorA, was implemented by the author. The other components were implemented by other team members of the WORKPAD project team.

Figure 4.9: WORKPAD Mobile GIS: Map View (left) and Context Menu (right)

4.2.4.1 WORKPAD Showcase Event

The WORKPAD project comprises a showcase event in the region of Calabria, Italy, in order to demonstrate the system, to verify its functionality, and to validate through user feedback. The mobile GIS application is one substantial part of this showcase. Several scenarios are prepared that shall exploit the WORKPAD modules. We present one of these scenarios subsequently and show how the GIS application is deployed.

Together with the user partners (Homeland Security Department of the region of Calabria) the following realistic scenario was established. The scenario is a prototypical example of a mobile collaboration application in emergency management.

A group of five firefighters (four team members plus one commander) needs to get an overview of an affected area after an earthquake in a city. They do not yet know if there are still people in the area who may potentially be hurt. In this case, they must immediately rescue them, give first aid, and make sure that necessary subsequent actions are initiated (like evacuation from the still dangerous area). To cover a greater area at a time the firefighters spread out. Suddenly, one firefighter detects close to him a burning lorry. After first investigations, he notices that there is still someone inside. He immediately notifies his colleagues by way of the commander. The commander needs to find out the location of the car and which tools and other team members are necessary as they all have different trainings and capabilities. One firefighter is already occupied with giving first aid to other wounded people. Although the other members are engaged too, their current tasks are of lower priority. As one possesses a portable fire extinguisher among his equipment and the other is specifically trained on first aid of burns both are notified to arrive at the burning car. The first firefighter who detected the car is already on site. The commander follows. Soon, all four firefighters are present and start conducting their activities. In parallel, the commander needs to find out where the closest vehicle is located to evacuate the rescued person. As soon as he knows he can contact the responsible authorities to send this vehicle to his current position. The car should arrive as soon as first aid is finished and the person is prepared for the transport. When all these activities are completed the group of the five firefighters continues with investigating the area.

The relevant occurring entities are modelled according to the W5 data model and in our implementation reflected as tuples in the tuple space federations. The W5 model already addresses most of the concepts of coordination theory, which makes it straightforward to model this mobile collaboration application according to W5 and comply with coordination theory.

According to the five entities of coordination theory, the *goals* would be the desired outcomes of the specific task, which in our example is on the one hand to get an overview of an affected area and on the other hand to rescue and evacuate all present people. The *actors* are the five firefighters, occurring vehicles, and other emergency operators on site. The *activities* are represented by the current and planned tasks of the actors as they are, in general, following specific action plans. Their specific capabilities and in particular their positions at specific times would be modelled as *constraints*. Also, the position of vehicles, for instance, would be *constraints*. These spatial constraints are Schelling Points. The *interdependencies* are related to constraints and show that one firefighter cannot conduct one activity he is not trained for or he is not capable of. Team members are interdependent as, for instance, there is a certain hierarchy and as they are spatially distributed and not available all the time. Also, different tasks are interdependent in the sense that they may have different priorities or the outcome of one task is input for another.

In order to allow appropriate information distribution and update among the actors CorA's tuple management and tuple distribution layers are deployed. Every actor is equipped with a portable device[7], which can also be only passively carried around (hence, for localisation purposes). These devices comprise computational capabilities, wireless communication means and a location sensor. Each device carries the local tuple spaces (at least the admin space and the generic space) which via replication consolidate to federated, quasi-global tuple space.

One particular coordination pattern is adopted in this example: the location-oriented coordination pattern as Schelling Points are evidently frequently occurring in such EM scenarios. This pattern is also designed integrating concepts of coordination theory. In our pattern implementation the coordination logic (i.e., the laws) is encapsulated in the `Actor` class in various methods (see Figure 3.11 in Section 3.2.1.5), hence, depicting a P2P system of actors communicating via distributed tuple spaces. The mobile GIS application represents the interface between this system and the user.

4.2.4.2 Benefits from Using CorA

The layered architecture of CorA was exploited as the underlying software system to facilitate the application development of that mobile geographic information system for portable devices. In the following we show how the functionalities of each layer of CorA was exploited.

Applying the Factual Data Layer
Real world facts that are relevant for the mobile geographic information system are represented by location information coming from GPS sensors. Examples for other facts are the text of annotations, particular information about particular points (points of interest), or status information about persons or objects.

Applying the W5 Data Model Layer
The W5 model is used to semantically combine relevant facts. If necessary, missing facts can also be inferred. The example on page 30 in Figure 3.6 clarify this idea better. In this case, the WHAT fact is inferred from the WHERE (a GPS position) and WHEN (a period of ten seconds) facts and embodies the status of the firefighter Smith which is "running".

Applying the Tuple Management Layer
In the mobile geographic information system we used two types of spaces that are available on each node in the network: one local space that keeps address information of the involved nodes (i.e., portable devices) and one local space that contains the application information which is mostly geographic information. This layer deals with the local interaction with these spaces, which is reading, writing, and deleting of W5 tuples via the APIs. All the tuples are stored and managed in the W5 format.

Applying the Tuple Distribution Layer
This layer is responsible for the network communication between the nodes, which is replication of new or modified tuples. This is accomplished in a decentralised mode, which implies circumventing the dependence on and drawback of a centralised single point of failure (such as a server).

---

[7]The reference devices in WORKPAD are the HTC TyTN-II and Sony Ericsson Xperia X1 PDAs.

Tuple replication is deployed according to various strategies. Address information, for instance, is always fully replicated at all times to all nodes. This is necessary because all nodes need to know how to reach the others. Full replication is feasible in this case because address information is comparatively lightweight—otherwise we could run into scalability problems. Other (geographic) information can be replicated in a context-sensitive manner. Location or status updates are only replicated to those nodes that really require that information.

Applying the Coordination Layer
Based on the framework provided by the coordination layer, the location-oriented coordination pattern was implemented and adopted in the mobile geographic information system. This pattern exploits spatial information for coordination. The theory behind that pattern was defined by Game Theorist and Nobel Prize winner Thomas C. Schelling, who discovered that people naturally orientate and coordinate based on distinct objects in time and space [149] (so-called Schelling Points). For more details about the concept of Schelling Points and the location-oriented coordination pattern we refer to Chapter 3.2.1.5 on page 43.

The *application layer* is merely the geography information viewer that invokes the APIs of CorA. Hence, it is not correct to talk about "applying" this layer.

4.3 Evaluation on User-Level

Within the course of WORKPAD two user tests were conducted [85]. The first test was an Internet-based online test. Mock-ups for each WORKPAD application were developed that showed the functionalities in principle. This test was used in order to better understand the users' needs and to get feedback whether the requirements have been understood correctly. The advantage of such mock-up tests is that developers and system engineers get a very early feedback about the intended component without having programmed anything potentially suboptimal. The mock-ups could be browsed on screen and the users were asked to fill in a subsequent questionnaire.

Thirteen users participated in that test[8]. Nine users were from the Calabrian Civil Protection Department, one from ANAS S.p.A., one from the Department of National Civil Protection, one from the Centre of Studi Peter of the Calabrian Civil Protection Department and one from KRONOS (Calabria/Academia Kronos). These test users in their daily work execute tasks like processing meteorological data, processing climate data, management activities, coordination of the Risk and Crisis Management sectors, logistics, hydrogeological risk monitoring, or risk prevention. 58% were male and 42% were female; 75% were between 31 and 45 years old, and 25% between 46 and 60.

The main results of the mock-up test regarding the mobile GIS application are summarized here. 85% of the users claimed that such an application is relevant and useful for their daily work. Ten users regarded the interface as comprehensive and intuitive. The real-time location indication is for five testers very useful and for six users useful. The presentation of grouped geographic information is for seven testers very much necessary

---

[8] According to [177], about 80% of potential usability problems can be discovered with five testers. Three testers would find the most severe problems. Also Nielsen confirmed that five users discover approximately 80% of usability problems [127]. With three testers it can be shown that 70% of usability problems could be found. Nielsen defined the law of "diminishing returns". He says that the third tester will do many things that have already been observed at the first or second user. Therefore the third tester generates only a small amount of new information. After the fifth user nothing really new is generated.

and for four necessary. The possibility of creating, annotating, and modifying relevant points-of-interest is for six testers very useful and for five useful.

Interesting is also the fact that one third of the users claimed that they need to actively coordinate activities with colleagues. Three users, moreover, stated that a mobile geographic information system is very usable for coordination activities; seven consider it as usable. As a coordination means nine testers prefer coordination by audio (such as telephone). Five users selected a "face-to-face" way of coordination, and four selected via radio communication technology. Only one user mentioned that it seems to be impossible to visually coordinate by a shared map and shared geographic information without any audio communication.

The second test within WORKPAD was a live test with eight users (pairs of two) in total using already real functional prototypes of the various WORKPAD applications. The users had to execute real tasks and for these use the software. In general, the feedback was positive. All users agreed that the software—if stable and mature enough—could support them in their daily work. The screen design of the real prototypes (see e.g. Figure 4.9 as an example) could be improved ("more attractive"). Particularly, regarding the mobile GIS application most of the users stated that it works without major difficulties and it is easy to use. The users appreciated the "position monitoring" and the possibility of real-time information exchange. As fields of improvements one outcome was that the used icons should be bigger. Also colours are significant. It is important to stick to the colour codes used by an emergency operations and to be consistent in that usage. Finally, the users state, it is essential that the software updates information fast and reliably. If only unreliable information is available, it is better not to present it as it may distract or confuse the operator, which might lead to wrong decisions.

Both user tests gave us very important feedback. It is natural that users, who are not system engineers and hence not familiar with internal technical details, judge what they see and experience. Hence, it is difficult to assess system services which are encapsulated in the middleware as users do not directly experience these. However, if users feel comfortable with a software system, as it is the case with the Mobile GIS application of WORKPAD, and do not complain about performance problems we can deduce that also CorA, which serves as the information distribution middleware that provides also the coordination pattern framework, is adequate for the target application area and audience.

4.4 Related Work

The Section introduces and discusses related works from the fields and disciplines relevant for this book. This Section, therefore, is subdivided into several topics:

1. Coordination in other disciplines

2. Tuple spaces

3. Software agents

4. Other related topics and paradigms

4.4.1 Coordination in Other Disciplines

Naturally, a lot of research effort on the topic of coordination is invested in the field of social sciences and related fields. "Collective Intelligence" of societies is one example that is very much related to coordination. In Section 2.1 Surowiecki's seminal work about the "Wisdom of Crowds" [163] was introduced. He investigates the establishment of collective opinions and decisions. He claims that "large groups of diverse individuals will make more intelligent decisions than even the most skilled decision-maker." For this opinion- and decision-making process he identifies three core problems. First, a problem with one definitive answer where information is missing and thus needs to be accurately assessed is referred to as a cognition problem (e.g., who will win an election, or what caused a disaster). Second, a problem that affects a whole group, where some sort of combination is necessary, and where this optimal solution is usually sought by having each individual act in personal self-interest is denoted as a coordination problem (e.g., determining the best route to work in traffic). This, indeed, is very similar to game theory considerations and to coordination games introduced in Section 2.1 on page 4. Third, a problem that is very similar to a coordination problem where the individuals, however, do not act in personal self-interest but the solution depends on individuals trusting each other and acting fairly. This problem is called cooperation problem (e.g., how to deal with pollution).

Another social scientist Philip H. Gulliver investigated disputes and negotiations between social entities [78]. For Gulliver, negotiations are closely related to coordination, which he defines as:

> Negotiations are processes of interaction between disputing parties whereby [...] they endeavor to come to an interdependent, joint decision concerning the terms of agreement on the issues between them. This joint decision is one that, in the end, is agreeable to and accepted by both parties after each has brought influence and persuasion to bear on the other [...] It often represents a compromise between the parties' initial demands and expectations.

In this definition the management of various interdependencies (e.g., individual goals, persuasions, or influences)—as this is how coordination is defined (see Definition 3)—is apparent. To conduct the process of negotiation, Gulliver proposes a so called Eight Phase model:

1. *Search for an arena*
   This implies the identification of the physical place where the negotiation can be conducted.

2. *Composition of an agenda and definition of issues*
   This is the definition of the environmental issues, the necessary requisites, and the etiquette.

3. *Establishing maximal limits to issues in dispute*
   This represents the first information exchange and tells the other party one's claims. It is the most antagonistic and competitive phase.

4. *Narrowing the differences*
   This is some form of reorientation. The parties try to discover if and where an agreement might be feasible.

5. *Preliminaries to final bargaining*
   Further clarifications are introduced in this phase. The final bargaining process is prepared. Unclarities have to be clarified. Each party has to know the other, what it wants and what it offers by now.

6. *Final bargaining*
   Proposals and counter-proposals are exchanged until the expectations of both parties converge and a decision is made.

7. *Ritual affirmation*
   This means a formal marking and sealing of the outcome (e.g., a contract).

8. *Execution of the agreement*
   Finally, the outcome has to be implemented—ideally immediately. One possibility is to pass the actual implementation to external parties or partners or let the implementation being monitored by them.

Gulliver also argues that basically every negotiation process no matter in which domain complies to those phases where some stages may possibly be skipped, which might be the case in many computer-based or agent-based negotiations. In [30], the authors adopted Gulliver's Eight Phase model of the negotiation process to a computer based system and could demonstrate its applicability to cooperating software agents.

Gulliver's works are a sub-set of what is called social network analysis [180] which is concerned with the investigation of particular configuration of nodes, their relationships and effects of such networks. From these analyses researchers expect novel insights which may as a consequence help to improve processes. A famous example concept that was discovered through social network analysis is the idea of the *six degrees of separation* as introduced on page 5 that led to the definition of the *small world* phenomenon. It says that everyone is an average of six contacts away from each person on Earth. In computer science, and in particular in computer supported process management and collaboration, the authors of [58] present an approach where social network analysis was adopted and exploited for deriving collaboration patterns. For this, ad-hoc business processes were analysed to gain more in-depth knowledge about inter-personal collaboration attitudes and to optimize accordingly.

In CorA, no structured social network analysis was conducted. The coordination architecture proposed, however, does incorporate well-known solutions to coordination patterns that have not been systematically investigated in this work but is derived from literature. The coordination patterns catalogue proposed in CorA is extensible and social network analysis—just as in [58] where collaboration patters were derived—seems to be a distinguished source for detection of further patterns.

A prerequisite for coordination activities and mechanisms are proper means of communication between coordinables (see Definition 7). The appropriate communication layers are encapsulated by middleware services. Various concepts and technologies related to the tuple space based approach of CorA are presented in the following section.

4.4.2 Tuple Spaces

As introduced in Section 3.2.1.3, the main middleware paradigm used in CorA for information distribution is the tuple space paradigm. Linda [69] was the first system using a central tuple space in order to store and distribute data. It was proposed that effective systems in the domain of parallel computing have to emphasize a high degree of decoupling among computing resources. The participants share information stored in a globally accessible, persistent data store, implemented as a centralized tuple space. Today similar space-based systems are (commercially) available such as JavaSpaces[9] [64], TSpaces[10] [103], GigaSpaces[11] [167], or XcoSpaces[12] which are based on the eXtensible Virtual Shared Memory (XVSM) technology [102].

The main difference of these systems compared to the decentralized space-based computing approach of CorA is the centralised server-based architecture representing a bottleneck and hampering flexibility, which is required by pervasive environments. Only later Linda implementations considered multiple spaces [87, e.g.]) but still in stationary networks. In CorA, we follow the distributed peer-to-peer based paradigm of decentralised tuple spaces with rich replication mechanisms.

A similar implementation of such an approach is LIME (Linda in a Mobile Environment)[13]. LIME [123, 138, 139] is a system that was built specifically to address mobility in a physical (i.e., devices) and logical (i.e., software agents) sense. Also in LIME, each host carries its own space. As soon as hosts are connected the available spaces are consolidated to a space federation similar to CorA. In LIME, this concept is called *transiently shared tuple spaces*. LIME also provides the possibility of defining reactions. A reaction can be viewed as a triple (ts, t, c) consisting of a tuple space reference ts, a template t and a code fragment c. The semantics of a reaction is that whenever a tuple matching t is deposited in ts, the code fragment c is executed. The main difference to CorA is that in a LIME network one primary copy of a tuple exists and the others are treated as replicas. CorA does not differentiate. Later works on LIME [121] provide the user with the possibility of defining replication profiles on a rather fine-grained level. In CorA, however, users only decide on one of the available strategies and the logics behind are transparent.

A subset of the LIME system is LighTS (Lightweight Tuple Space) [137] which is the underlying Java-based tuple space implementation of LIME. The design goal of LighTS was minimality and extensibility with a focus on providing support for basic Linda operations in a local implementation of a tuple space which can be used directly (e.g., for supporting coordination among co-located agents). More sophisticated distribution mechanisms need to be implemented on top of LighTS. In CorA, we actually exploit parts of LighTS for the fundamental space operations. As CorA targets at Java 2 Micro Edition (J2ME) platform Connected Limited Device Configuration (CLDC), the original LighTS, which does only provide a very limited implementation, had to be fundamentally extended.

Other extensions or continuations of LIME are TinyLIME and TeenyLIME. TinyLime is an extension of Lime for the sensor network environment [46]. It extends LIME by providing features and middleware components specialized for sensor networks. An implementation is available for the Crossbow Mote[14] sensor technology. In TinyLIME the major parts of the programming logic is placed on the sinks that collect sensor data. In TeenyLIME [45], however, more intelligence is encapsulated by the sensor nodes themselves, thus, embodying a more decentralised sensor network architecture. TeenyLIME is designed for scenarios where the application intelligence is in the network, built around node-to-node interactions inside a wireless sensor network and for this introduces novel concepts such as range matching, capability tuples, freshness, and explicit control over reliability which are neither available in LIME nor in TinyLIME [45]. CorA is different to TinyLIME as the

---
[9]See http://www.jini.org/wiki/JavaSpaces_Specification
[10]See http://www.almaden.ibm.com/cs/TSpaces/
[11]See http://www.gigaspaces.com/
[12]See http://www.xcoordination.com/
[13]See http://lime.sourceforge.net/
[14]See http://www.xbow.com/

notion of a sink is not necessary. The coordination is entirely decentralised in a P2P fashion. In contrast to TeenyLIME, we assume that the CorA framework is more general and not optimised for one sensor platform, which clearly comes with the cost of being more heavyweight and hence not deployable on any sensors which are potentially too resource restricted. Parts of CorA have experimentally been deployed on SunSPOT[15] sensors (see Section 4.5 for details).

Limone (Lightly-coordinated Mobile Network) [63]—similar to LIME—supports logically mobile agents and physically mobile hosts. Limone assumes an agent-centric perspective on coordination by allowing each agent to dene its own acquaintance policy and by limiting all agent-initiated interactions to agents that satisfy the policy. Each agent can maintain an acquaintance list and coordination is only necessary between relevant peers. Limone tailors Linda-like primitives for mobile environments by eliminating remote blocking and complex group operations. The policies of group interactions in CorA are configured by using one of the four replication strategies. In a context-dependent replication strategy the receiving peers can be configured. Hence, a flooding of the network can be avoided.

In CoreLime [33] the authors claim to overcome some limitations in LIME regarding efficiency, scalability, atomicity, and security. Their proposal is to have agent mobility as the only mean of information distribution. Hence, they describe a revised LIME model that does not provide remote tuple operations in order to overcome deficiencies in the original specification and implementation of LIME. CorA does not support code or agent mobility. In CorA we also decided to support only one type of mobility. In our case it is physical mobility. Presumably, the CorA framework is more heavyweight than CoreLime (due to rich replication mechanisms). However, CorA from the beginning was tailored to mobile collaboration of teams with a small team size, where we could show the appropriateness.

Similar to CoreLime, the Mobile Agent Reactive Spaces (MARS) [32] provide logically mobile agents that migrate from one execution environment to another. A local tuple space is associated with each execution environment, where agents can store and retrieve messages in a spatial and temporal uncoupled way. MARS is programmable, meaning that agents can associate reactions to the operations made on the space. An agent can only coordinate with other agents that reside on the same node. Agent migration is required for inter-node communication.

TuCSoN (Tuple Centres over the Network) [133] is a coordination model intended to be associated with existing agent systems. Every host provides tuple spaces that can be used by local agents for inter-agent communication and to access local resources. Tuple spaces have unique names at the host level, and Linda like operations can be performed remotely on them by specifying their name and the name of the host. In addition, TuCSoN extends tuple spaces with the notion of behaviour specification, which are similar to reactions. Coordination artifacts [132] are used for coordinating agents via the mediation of a space containing such artifacts. Coordination artifacts are types of objects that represent basic units of coordination and that, by encapsulating behaviour other than data, can effectively embody coordination laws and can effectively act as virtual representations of objects and facts of the real world. In CorA a similar effect can be achieved by exploiting W5 tuples. Due to their uniform structuring, these are more suitable for open and dynamic interactions than general, unstructured, artifacts. Still, W5 tuples cannot embody behaviour and functions, which have to be encapsulated in other layers of CorA. In our view, this is a different way of enforcing separation

---

[15]See http://www.sunspotworld.com/

of concerns between the factual data layer and the layer of coordination laws.

The KLAIM (Kernel Language for Agents Interaction and Mobility) model [53] also supports logical mobility or code migration, using locality-aware tuple spaces to provide a means for inter-process communication. KLAIM processes located at a given location communicate through a co-located tuple space. There is no transient sharing among several tuple spaces—as in our coordination architecture or in LIME—but a process can interact with any tuple space by identifying its locality. An integral part of the KLAIM model is also the specification of process migration but instead does not explicitly address tuple replication issues.

Another tuple space system is embodied by the tuples-on-the-air (TOTA) approach [111]. TOTA allows interactions to occur via tuple exchanges, too. For this, tuples are injected into the network and propagate through the network on a temporal and spatial scale. Context-sensitive distribution rules can be defined and associated with tuples. Hence, the TOTA middleware propagates tuples across a network on the basis of application-specific patterns and adapts the resulting distributed structures accordingly to changes in the network topology. Applications can query the tuple distribution structures and exploit them to acquire contextual information and carry on complex coordination activities in an adaptive way. This approach offers more flexibility as basically any strategy of propagation (i.e., replication) can be accomplished. However, this comes with certain costs: First, every node carrying a tuple space must know and maintain the network topology over at least the next couple of hops. Second, the application—when creating a tuple—must define the propagation rules, which is rather unmanageable. In CorA, simply one out of four pre-defined replication strategies can be chosen to get the same effects.

In the Event Heap project [94, 95] the authors recognised the appropriateness of tuple spaces for room-based pervasive computing environments, which they denote as "interactive workspaces". These are environments where people come together and perform collaborative activities such as design review or brainstorming. In the Event Heap system, tuples are referred to as *events*, which "reflects their intended use as a means of notifying other applications in the workspace of an occurrence, or of requesting that other applications update their state or perform some task" [94]. The tuple space model is extended by interesting new features beneficial for room-based collaboration, namely self-description of tuples, tuple sequencing (to overcome the non-deterministic nature of tuple matching operations), expiration of tuples (a form of garbage collection to avoid a overflow of unnecessary tuples), default routing fields (to allow a targeted routing of particular tuples to dedicated receivers), and query registration (similar to a publish/subscribe mechanism where a registered agent is notified about a tuple it is interested in). These extensions are not entirely new as they have already been mentioned by other research work. New, however, is the application area (room-based collaboration) and this particular combination and integration as shown in Event Heap. As opposed to CorA, Event Heap is a centralised system that is dependent on a server controlling the tuple space. Interactive workspace applications need to connect in a client/server fashion. Most of the extensions to classic tuple spaces of Event Heap are as functionalities also available in CorA, such as the self-description of tuples, expiration of tuples (encapsulated in the *Whatabout* field of W5 tuples), or query registration (can be accomplished by the push mode of the context-dependent replication strategy). Also, Event Heap addresses another type of collaborative applications, namely those where participants are geographically co-located. Whereas, CorA focuses on spatially and temporally different collaboration (see also taxonomy presented in Figure 3.1 on page 13).

The authors of L^{2}imbo [11, 179] propose that all communication of applications in mobile, heterogeneous environments should be done by tuple spaces. Hence, they focus on providing inter-application communication through different tuple spaces entailing different quality-of-service (QoS) channels. Applications can subscribe to those tuple spaces that most closely match their QoS requirements (e.g., bandwidth) for communication. The L^{2}imbo system is composed of a freely determinable configuration of local, central, and distributed tuple spaces over a network of possibly mobile nodes. The really novel contribution to the tuple space paradigm of L^{2}imbo are the QoS attributes that can be assigned to tuples: deadlines (for tuple (re-)ordering), priorities (for classifying tuples according to urgency), and cost (for determining the cost of propagating a tuple over expensive network links). L^{2}imbo provides the necessary API abstraction to define the necessary QoS policy on a tuple basis. We would consider the L^{2}imbo system as addressing more low-level network management functionalities than CorA. CorA is closer to the application level. Hence, both systems could potentially be exploited in complementary fashion, where CorA may run over L^{2}imbo. This, however, may not be possible without adaptations as presumably some redundancies (regarding redundant tuple space operations) may arise.

Another tuple space middleware is EgoSpaces described in [96], which is based on the LIME model. It is a context-aware middleware that deploys tuple spaces but without any pre-defined context dimensions as in our architecture. The notion of *views* was introduced denoting an individualized and egocentric projection of all data available to one specific reference agent. This is a beneficial concept as the large amount of data can be tailored to the real specific needs of an agent according to its current context. Such a mechanism is not explicitly provided in our data model but similar results can be acquired through context-dependent queries formulated by peers. Schelfthout et al. [147] define *views* based on the network connectivity within a MANET specifying context as the configuration of participating nodes and the corresponding available data. They use ObjectPlaces [148] as the coordination middleware to manage context which is subject to change because information on reachable nodes changed, or the set of reachable nodes itself changed.

XMLSpaces [172] bring together the common communication format XML with the coordination language Linda. It aims at providing coordination in Web-based cooperative information systems. XML documents are represented as one-fielded tuples where the relations amongst XML files can be used for matching. Generally, XMLSpaces use a centralised architecture with a server controlling the XMLSpaces. These spaces, additionally, can be distributed to span several servers at different locations but logically form one consistent data space.

Semantic Web Spaces [171, 173] extend the concept of XMLSpaces such that they are capable of processing and exploiting Semantic Web technologies. In essence, semantic technologies are combined with tuple space technology, which is also referred to as triple space computing [60]. In XMLSpaces, content is structured according to an XML tree. The structure of a Semantic Web Space is represented explicitly by means of an ontology (model of the tuple space). The ontology describes the typical components of the tuple space, such as sub-spaces, supported tuple types and matching templates, and coordinates the information access. Syntactically, knowledge in Semantic Web Spaces is represented by the Resource Description Framework (RDF) documents and statements. A knowledge "item" in triple spaces, hence, is represented by a triple with the structure (`subject, predicate, object`). By re-using the object of one statement as the subject of another, the tuple space can build a semantic graph structure of the contained knowledge. Several different types of tuple spaces are considered: RDFSpaces (stores RDF triples), OWLSpaces (to permit the use of OWL (Web Ontology Language) concepts), RuleSpaces (to generate interaction laws), ReasonSpaces (to provide means for logical reasoning), and TrustSpaces (to allow authentication mechanisms). Fensel [60] claimed that triple space technology "may become the web for machines as the web based on HTML became the Web for humans".

XMLSpaces as well as its successor Semantic Web Spaces embody heavyweight concepts and, thus, seem to be more appropriate for stationary, Web-based collaboration. Nevertheless, the advantage of semantic technologies are apparent and worth an investigation in the context of CorA and mobile collaboration but are out of scope of this research work. Due to the open structure of the W5 data model adopted in CorA it could be extended to integrate XML-type data (such as RDF). A beneficial consequence of integrating semantic technologies would be the possibility to conduct more sophisticated reasoning and inferring, which is of relevance in any scenario.

In this Section we discussed tuple space based middleware systems similar to CorA that embody most of the coordination logic. Another design approach is to move this coordination logic (or intelligence) away from the environment and encapsulate it in the acting entities. These entities are software pieces that are also referred to as intelligent agents. The next Section introduces relevant agent technologies and concepts.

4.4.3 Software Agents

Agent technology has already been touched in Section 3.1.1[16]. Due to the autonomy of agents in an agent system, proper coordination is a crucial aspect. Nwana defines coordination in an agent-based system as the "process in which agents engage in order to ensure a community of individual agents acts in a coherent manner" [130]. This means that the agents within a system have to behave like one unit in order to achieve their common higher goal. The authors of [91] and [130] point out why coordination among agents is essential:

- Preventing anarchy and chaos which is an inherent property of a collection of autonomous equivalent entities
- Meeting global constraints which are entailed by the properties and boundary of the system in existence
- Accessing distributed expertise, resources, information and knowledge
- Resolving dependencies between agents' actions which are often interdependent
- Enhancing efficiency by parallel processing and collaboration

These points are a direct result of proper coordination, thus resulting in coordination being an indispensable premise for collaboration.

Coordination is an abstract and complex process particularly occurring in social networks. By regarding agents as socially competent [186], sociality can be incorporated into agent-based systems. Nwana differentiates between the following four coordination techniques [130]:

- *Organizational structuring:* All the components of a coordination system such as actors, activities, constraints, interdependencies, and goals but also the different roles, point in time of changing this role, the communication paths, the relationships and the strategy to resolve the interdependencies are defined in a hierarchical structure denoted as an organization. Hence, the whole coordination process is thoroughly defined a priori, which implies intensive preparation efforts and a very static behaviour of the coordination system during runtime.

---
[16] See also the according Definition 9 on page 129.

- *Multi-agent planning:* A predefined plan of action is available and a centralised agent responsible for the coordination of the components is present. This agent requires global knowledge to a large extent, which represents a major problem in highly distributed systems of fairly autonomous entities like agent-based systems. This technique is regarded as an a priori definition type.

- *Contracting:* During runtime, a superior instance breaks problems down into sub-problems, searches for task-solving entities, and sets up a contract with them about the completion (e.g. Contract Net Protocol [160]). These superior instances, the problems to be solved, the strategy to break these down into sub-problems, and the subsequent distribution are defined a priori. Nevertheless, most of the decisions are made during runtime resulting in more flexibility in reacting to changing circumstances like sudden unattainability of various mobile entities.

- *Negotiation:* By using this technique, coordination is accomplished by negotiating and bargaining—meaning the repeated exchange of proposals and counter-proposals—about how to resolve interdependencies such as the mutual need of a specific resource. The outcome, eventually, is in most cases a compromise [93]. This type is a representative where the coordinative system behaves completely in an ad hoc way.

Software agents can be classified from very simple, tropistic agents that simply react to external stimulus to intelligent agents. The more intelligent the more challenging is the coordination. One example of an intelligent agent approach are the *Beliefs-Desires-Intentions* (BDI) agents [140] which incorporate Michael Bratman's theory of human practical reasoning [24]. The beliefs represent the informational state of the agent internally. This is what the agent knows about its world. The desires represent the motivational state of the agent. These are the goals an agent wants to achieve. The intentions represent the deliberative state of the agent. These are the actions an agents plans to execute in order to satisfy its desires. Later, this BDI approach was extended by commitments and conventions (BDI-C) [90]. Commitments are (mutual) promises among agents about undertaking a specific course of actions. Conventions provide a means of monitoring commitments in changing circumstances. Both are beneficial for coordination among BDI agents but are more related to the agency (i.e., the environment an agent is embedded in). Hence, commitments and conventions are a type of a meta coordination mechanism that is not decentrally controlled by the autonomous agents but is a concept that is either distributed over all relevant agents (which requires expensive coordination for itself) or situated in the environment (which may be considered as contradicting the idea of intelligent agents postulating that the intelligence is encapsulated in agents).

Many other agent systems [31, 122, e.g.] deal with the coordination issue in problem-specific and target-oriented ways and thus, are too proprietary and not generally applicable. An example is workflow and business process modelling. Workflows within an enterprise are very complex and multifarious. ADEPT [93] is one representative project that developed the technology of negotiating agents for agent-enabled workflow modelling. ADEPT was developed for and with the British Telecom (BT) and its aim was to provide customers with a quote about the costs of installing a computer network meeting the customer's requirements. The whole workflow within BT was identified and consequently, autonomous problem solving entities (i.e. agents) were designed. Several BT departments (e.g. customer service, design, legal etc.), some external involved contractors and also each individual of each department were all represented by agents. Thus, the whole business organization was modelled as an agent-based system comprising a society of service providing, service consuming, negotiating and mediating agents, resulting in many diverse communication behaviours and organizational structures like C/S, P2P, master-slave, blackboard, group etc. To achieve the overall goal, every agent had to interact with others, hence, producing many proposals and counter-proposals until the final contract was negotiated and approved and the quote was delivered to the customer. ADEPT was not implemented as a generic agent-based system but very purpose-oriented and specific to workflow and business process management. It was based on the CORBA middleware technology, which dealt with the distributed and heterogeneous resources and entities of the system. The legacy system like various databases were incorporated by building a wrapper around those parts, which represented the interface to the agent-based system and did the two-way translation of the information. The functionality of the ADEPT system can be easily extended by simply adding further agents encapsulating the desired functions. Artificial Intelligence was basically used for the negotiation processes [158].

Strictly speaking, software agents are autonomous and act on the behalf of their (human) user [106–108]. This is not the case in CorA. In CorA, the system supports users in their mobile collaboration activities. Nevertheless, many concepts out of the software agents world are relevant for CorA and can be found on various abstraction layers. In particular, at CorA's coordination layer where coordination laws are combined and abstracted to patterns autonomous software components can be identified. In the supervisor/worker pattern, for instance, supervisors and workers may represent such components.

So far, we discussed three major related topics (coordination in other disciplines, tuple spaces, and software agents). The research work necessary for CorA, however, is related to many more areas and research fields. In the following section we summarize several of the most important.

4.4.4 Other Related Topics

The research work presented in this book touches several other and diverse topics and relevant research areas. One such area is context-aware computing. Most of the related work has been focusing on acquiring individual pieces of contextual information and less on making it available in a more formalized model [153]. As a consequence, due to the lack of expressive models, complex pervasive situations cannot be effectively processed. More structured approaches to modelling context considering sets of environmental variables which can be queried [151], or structured models in which contextual information can be aggregated and enriched by features related to information imperfection, e.g., temporal aspects [81] are required. These approaches tend to make the context model quite complex, and it is difficult to effectively manage services based on these models. The W5 concept exploited in CorA avoids this problem by structuring all characteristics of the context in five well-defined fields. A similar proposal in [38] adopts a seven-field data structure to describe the context, four of which corresponding to our W5 fields. However, the purpose is for managing consistency between data from multiple and heterogeneous sources rather than to support context for collaboration activities.

Context-sensitive data structures (CSDS) [136] provide a unified interface to contextual information. This interface concept is similar as in W5. In CSDS, context items are defined as pieces of data generated by agents. Every agent, however, can generate its own CSDS describing his current context arbitrarily. We believe that it is more beneficial to specify a certain structure a priori (as the five fields in W5) in order to facilitate interoperability between heterogeneous systems.

The semantics of the W5 concept are simple and extensible (e.g., by namespaces), which due to adaptability we consider as a strength. Another approach would be the Context Ontology Language (CoOL) [162], which uses the Aspect-Scale-Context model where each aspect can have several scales to express context. This approach is especially useful for quantifying and converting but may suffer from being constricted and inflexible.

In [48], a similar concept to model context as in W5 was presented. The work, however, particularly focuses on the context modelling by using well-defined and established ontologies for e-learning scenarios. CorA, instead, discusses a more comprehensive approach also covering the necessary infrastructure (i.e., middleware services).

Apart from context-aware computing, sensing and integration of the (physical as well as virtual) environment is an essential aspect in CorA. Weyns et al [183] propose to let the environment participate as an active entity to allow for subjective (i.e., intra-agent dependencies towards other agents) as well as objective coordination (i.e., inter-agent coordination issues external to the agents related to the environment the agent is embedded in). As argued in [17], the coordination logic can be encapsulated somewhere on an axis between the environment and the coordinable (e.g., agent), which depends highly on the intended application. The environment in CorA is not modelled as an additional active entity but it is integrated by peers sensing and actuating or changing the environment in order to leave cues which can be exploited by other peers.

In Computer Science in general, mathematical formalisms play an important role for describing and proving systems and for estimating their behaviours. CorA was described by adopting Mobile UNITY (see Section 3.2.2) but several other mathematical formalisms would be feasible. One widely used formalisms is the π-calculus [119], which is used to describe processes and communication between processes. Although more than 15 years ago when it was originally developed, it was designed to accommodate mobile processes. But rather in the sense of that the mobility of processes is expressed by their change over time. There is no concept of location in π-calculus which is the key in CorA's formalization.

Another alternative would be the deployment of Situation Calculus as in the ConGolog [49] formalism. It was originally designed to model dynamically changing domains of interest or situations. In [50], this Situation Calculus was exploited to formalize an adaptive process management system in dynamic and pervasive situations (in the context of emergency management). Clearly, location is one parameter of such changing situations. But also this formalism does not explicitly provide spatial concepts.

In [29], Busi et al define a process algebra for Linda coordination primitives called LINPA (LINda Process Algebra). This approach is based on CCS[17] [117] process calculus which was also the base groundwork for the π-calculus. Although LINPA represents a significant contribution to tuple space operation formalization it is at this stage too much focused on modelling basic operations and basic coordination primitives. The formalization attempt presented in our work goes beyond these operation and requires richer concepts from the formalism, which was provided by Mobile UNITY.

After this analysis and comparison of CorA with several related work efforts, we continue with the second major part of this section with is the interpretation of CorA's behaviour and performance in various tests stemming from the system design. We also critically reflect the approach and outline future exploitations and prospects.

---

[17]Calculus of Communicating Systems.

4.5 Interpretation and Reflection

We started this research work with the idea of causing a positive effect in engineering of pervasive information system systems for mobile collaboration by explicitly considering coordination theory. The expected effect was to discover an optimisation potential that lies in the way coordination is handled.

The course of examination of this problem statement we developed a coordination architecture for pervasive environments for which we respected coordination theory (the definition of coordination and the five coordination entities as presented in Section 2). The proposed system comprises three core elements: decoupled and opportunistic communication, pattern-based coordination, and a data model that is capable of processing context. Various verification methods—on system-, developer-, and user-level—were adopted for evaluating the presented research work. The following paragraphs summarize these methods and interpret the results.

One contribution of this research work is the development of a coordination model for pervasive environments that takes into account the related characteristics. We took considerations from coordination theory and integrated them into our model. Our model, finally, subsumes a definition of coordination that is adapted for pervasive environments (see Definition 3 on page 129) and the five coordination entities. These are goals, actors, activities, constraints, and interdependencies. This coordination model can be exploited for an initial break down and structuring of coordination problems. In Section 4.2, we demonstrated the application of this model to mobile collaboration scenarios in emergency management in the scope of the European research project WORKPAD. The scenario presented on pages 107ff was structured and discussed by exploiting this coordination model.

The system design of the implemented coordination architecture CorA is also based on this model, which led to the various architectural layers that serve for a separation of concerns. CorA embodies concepts that particularly address the requirements of pervasive information systems, which were analysed through a scenario based elicitation. We exploited the structured but open W5 data model, which is covered by CorA's data model layer, for integrating data coming from the real world with data coming from the virtual world. At the same time, context is modelled by using W5, and context is the major source of the *constraints* coordination entity.

A further concept of CorA that addresses the communication requirements is the adoption of distributed tuple spaces for optimal information distribution. Disconnections in pervasive environments are the rule—not the exception as in stationary environments. Hence, communication must be decoupled and opportunistic [112], which is given by the distributed tuple spaces paradigm. This paradigm clearly has its limits as decentralised approaches always involve a higher communication effort and, thus, more traffic than centralised systems (cf. P2P versus C/S) and the communication links in pervasive environments are naturally wireless and offer less bandwidth and throughput. Nevertheless, the target application area is mobile collaboration. In general, literature suggests that more meaningful and more effective collaboration is performed with less participants [12]. In particular, the team size in emergency management is not larger then ten team members. Teams are usually aggregated to larger teams but the smallest unit is always a group of less then ten. This is what we targeted at with the design of the information distribution component of CorA. Two layers are responsible for information distribution: the tuple management layer and tuple distribution layer. The tuple management layer deals with basic tuple space interactions on the local spaces of a peer. The tuple distribution layer encapsulates the distribution of tuple to various relevant peers through configurable replication mechanisms. With respect to behaviour metrics of information distribution we measured scalability and consistency. The system tests presented in Section 4.1 show—with five participating peers—a standard deviation of 0.43 different tuples over all spaces at a time, and 4.43 with ten participating peers. The so called consistency time span (i.e., the time it takes until consistency over all spaces is reached again) is in the first test case 3.49 seconds and in the second case 8.75 seconds. Five to ten participants is a realistic number in mobile collaboration scenarios in emergency management. Combining the results of both test cases adds up to an average standard deviation of 2.43 and an average consistency time span of 6.12. Consequently, on average 0.39 tuples are inconsistent per second. In other words, one inconsistent tuple occurs in a space every three seconds. Based on these results we conclude that the scalability and consistency metrics are sufficient for the target applications.

In addition, the various replication strategies provided by the tuple distribution layer were formally described by using the Mobile UNITY notation. This formal description and related reasoning laid the foundation for the implementation of the strategies. In fact, the formalization and implementation iteratively altered and influenced each other. With the help of the formalized strategies, formulae were derived that help to estimate the replication costs (i.e., the number of necessary transmissions) of a strategy in a particular situation a priori.

The next layer above the tuple distribution layer is the coordination layer that is concerned with providing mechanisms to resolve interdependencies, which essentially is defined as coordination (see Definition 3 on page 129). Our goal was to subsume and abstract several such mechanisms to, eventually, provide standard solutions to recurring coordination problems. This is called a coordination pattern. In CorA we provide a catalogue of several such patterns. Through the adoption of CorA to the Mobile GIS application of WORKPAD as presented in Section 4.2 we could show the modularity and ease of integration of various layers of CorA for mobile collaboration applications. In WORKPAD, we exploited the location-oriented coordination pattern and visualised this concept by using digital maps on portable devices that display real-time information such as positions of relevant persons or objects, or annotations on the map related to points-of-interest. The approach was also evaluated through various tests by users who gave us positive feedback and pointed out fields of improvements (see Section 4.2.4 on page 109).

To summarize, on a developer-view, CorA can be exploited to build pervasive computing applications that require coordinated information distribution between several mobile nodes more effectively. Due to the functionalities encapsulated in the CorA middleware opportunities arise that cannot be accomplished in a similar way with conventional (mostly centralised) approaches that require a stationary hardware environment. The system behavior regarding scalability and consistency time span is at least for human collaboration scenarios sufficient. From a user-view, the mobile geographic information application that is based on CorA exhibit a great user acceptance and satisfaction rate. No major critics were encountered which leads to the conclusion that CorA is an adequate middleware solution for such types of pervasive applications. With CorA, we additionally provide best-practise recommendations in the form of pattern based problem solutions. Users can exploit these patterns to solve daily coordination problems.

From the interpretations of the results of various verification methods we deduce that explicitly considering coordination theory in engineering of systems for collaboration support in pervasive environments *has* a positive effect on users engaged in mobile collaboration scenarios. Their effectiveness can be improved because decision making processes can be improved by providing more knowledge faster, without unambiguity and also visually as opposed to the modus operandi of emergency operators of today who use voice over (mostly analogue) radio communication. Knowledge can be brought to the user through the distributed tuple space based information distribution mechanisms of CorA. Efficiency can be increased by exploiting coordination that is based on a coordination model for pervasive environments and, hence, optimised for mobile collaboration. An optimisation potential lies in collaborative scenarios and can be addressed by explicitly dealing with coordination.

As a critical reflection, in CorA some important topics such as security or usability have not been explicitly addressed as they are considered out of scope of the book. One might, for instance, argue that applications based on CorA may suffer from a bad usability and, hence, will never be accepted by users. Just consider a firefighter who usually wears gloves. It would be inappropriate to equip him with a portable device such as a PDA. On the one hand, there are definitely many situations where a PDA as an interface to a computer-based system is useful for a firefighter (e.g., training, preparation, or documentation tasks). On the other hand, the focus of CorA clearly was the engineering of a middleware system. Applications and their interfaces build up on top of CorA and, hence, are out of scope. We used the PDA merely as one example interface. Many research efforts are going on that investigate wearable computing[18] which facilitate the integration of unobtrusive and convenient user interface into clothes.

CorA as a framework is rather broad and touches various topics. For instance, communication and quality of service issues might have been implemented better in other projects. Again because QoS was not the focus of CorA. In L^2imbo, the authors concentrated on providing a QoS configurable communication middleware that is optimised for different types of traffic. Nevertheless, due to the modularity of CorA it is possible to exchange layers. If the L^2imbo system is still available a combination with CorA shall be feasible. Beneficial effects must be examined.

A further critique may be the fact that CorA only considers small groups of users. This is justified, however, to the best of the knowledge of the author no other system that scales up to a higher number of users in the same context of mobile collaboration is available. The problem is a general one as we have to do a balancing act between, on the one hand, centralised systems (client/server) which are not flexible enough and, on the other hand, decentralised solutions (P2P) which require a higher traffic load due to more complex information distribution. Higher traffic load, in turn, results in limits with respect to scalability and (wireless) transmission technology capabilities. On the contrary, as argued earlier, mobile collaboration is more effective with a smaller team size and we could show the applicability of the approach at least in one representative application example in emergency management. In our tests we deployed the full replication strategy which is the most "expensive" one and showed that the consistency, scalability, and performance behaviours between five and ten users is acceptable. By deploying more economical strategies, where the appropriateness always depends on the situation, the figures improve.

The developments related to CorA and WORKPAD will be further exploited. Based on the outcomes, in our research group we envisage the extension to a more comprehensive and modular *Mobile Collaboration Toolkit* that subsumes several software pieces that can be composed as needed for particular projects or products related to (mobile) collaboration. As one of the next extensions we foresee the integration of sensor networks. CorA's distributed tuple spaces shall we deployable on sensors and exploited to propagate sensor values through a network of possibly mobile sensors.

---

[18]See research projects for example http://www.wearitatwork.com, http://www.media.mit.edu/wearables/, or http://www.snow-project.org/

Due to the experiences regarding mobile geographic information systems (GIS) one integral part of that toolkit will be a GeoCollaboration framework, which we already work on. GeoCollaboration denotes any collaborative activity supported through the use of geo-information technologies. Mobile collaboration can be significantly supported through spatial information and geographic analysis [15] what we also experienced with the WORKPAD mobile GIS application.

With this toolkit for mobile collaboration applications we follow the trends towards pervasive information systems as we discussed it early in this work (Section 3.1.1). As technology matures also people and their way of exploiting services changes. In the future the frequency of pervasive service invocation and exploitation will increase. Mobile collaboration represents one type of such pervasive services. We are living in the Information Age and mankind never produced so much information as today. Knowledge is based on information. In fact, knowledge is information that is processed, filtered, and applied to a special situation—thus, resulting in knowledge relevant for a particular knowledge consuming entity in a particular context. A major challenge of the future will be proper coordination of knowledge in order to provide users with knowledge that is relevant for their context, which is of particular importance in pervasive environments [22][19].

4.6 Chapter Summary

After the preceding Chapter 3 described implementation details of the coordination language based on the concepts of CorA, this Chapter presented the results of various experiments conducted. We differentiated between three levels of experiments. First, we quantitatively tested the system behaviour of the middleware by performing two test cases with different test set-ups. Both were executed twice and the results (also with calculated average values) were illustrated. During these tests we focused on the two system behaviour metrics scalability and consistency. A satisfying behaviour of the middleware (indicated by these two metrics) is the essential prerequisite for the appropriate performance of the system and the later acceptance by the user. Appropriate information distribution provided by the middleware is inevitable for the claimed increase in effectiveness and efficiency.

Second, we qualitatively assessed the applicability of CorA on a developers view by exploiting them in the context of the European research project WORKPAD which deals with mobile collaboration applications in the domain of emergency management. We tested the ease of integration of CorA into another system. For this, we exploited several layers of the CorA architecture and one coordination pattern.

Third, we assessed the user satisfaction by performing several user tests who gave us feedback about the resulting WORKPAD application that included parts of CorA. This qualitative evaluation represented a further verification method on a users' view.

In addition we confronted the approaches taken in CorA with related works and highlighted the differences and their implications. We discussed coordination in several other disciplines on a broader basis such as coordination in social science. As the information distribution mechanisms in CorA are distributed tuple spaces

---

[19]In order to discuss the issue on coordination of knowledge with other researchers we organized a dedicated workshop on *Coordination Models and Applications (CoMA): Knowledge in Pervasive Environments*. See `http://mowi.salzburgresearch.at/wetice`, where the topics covered by CorA were of high relevance.

we presented many of such systems that offer diverse characteristics and advantages. As agent systems comprise social networks, coordination is of prime importance there, too. We presented the most essential concepts of coordination in multi agent systems. Finally, we combined several topics still relevant but of minor importance and show some approaches there, too.

The experiments and the confrontation with related work serve as the basis for the subsequent interpretation and discussion. In the last part of this Chapter we interpreted the various methods we adopted for verifications.

We could show that CorA's information distribution is appropriate for the target scenarios. We exploited the coordination model (the definition of coordination in pervasive environments and the five coordination entities) as the basis for devising the coordination architecture CorA and for modelling the WORKPAD mobile collaboration application example of emergency management. As an example, we used one coordination pattern of CorA (location-oriented coordination) as the basis for a mobile collaboration application that integrates digital maps and geographic information (GeoCollaboration). By aggregating the results of the various verification methods we concluded that an optimisation potential can be exploited by explicitly addressing coordination.

The next Chapter is the final one and concludes this research work by summarizing the main ideas about exploiting coordination and outlining future directions.

Chapter 5

Coordination and Beyond

The intention of this book was to make coordination concepts explicit and to reveal its optimisation potential. If coordination concepts are explicitly addressed (as by definition) the interdependencies can be resolved in a more efficient way, thus leading to utilising the optimisation potential. This is a general approach and not only valid for a minority of cases. Coordination is omnipresent and can be identified in many different facets and in most diverse regards.

In order to make our approach easier to comprehend we presented the concrete showcase of applying coordination to a domain. For this we designed and developed an IT based system for which we respected coordination mechanisms already in the system design. We called the resulting system the coordination architecture CorA and applied it to collaboration scenarios of mobile users in emergency management cases.

From the results presented in this book, we could show that our approach of explicitly addressing coordination mechanisms in the design of applications intended for pervasive environments has a positive effect. Our evaluations showed that with this approach and architecture design we can very effectively deal with the specific characteristics of pervasive environments. The system behavior regarding scalability and consistency time span is at least for human collaboration scenarios sufficient. Due to the functionalities encapsulated in the CorA middleware opportunities arise that cannot be accomplished in a similar way with conventional (mostly centralised) approaches that require a stationary hardware infrastructure.

On a developer-view, CorA can be exploited to build pervasive computing applications that require coordinated information distribution between several mobile nodes more effectively by invoking available functionality. The various layers can be deployed as required in a flexible way. New coordination patterns can be developed and integrated or available ones can be availed on-demand. Developers can profit from CorA due to its ease of applicability, re-usability, and extensibility leading to more efficient system development.

From a user's point of view, the mobile geographic information application that is based on CorA and represents the actual interface between the user and the CorA coordination middleware exhibits a good user acceptance and satisfaction rate. No major critics were encountered which leads to the conclusion that CorA is an adequate middleware solution for such types of pervasive applications. Mobile emergency operators stated that with such a system new opportunities arise that make executing their activities much more efficient. For instance, being informed about the position and status of their colleagues in real-time without the need of explicitly asking helps to make their processes faster and easier. In other words, it help to *optimise* their work.

This is, however, only one perspective of coordination that we showed in this book in order to make the concept and the potential more tangible. IT can help to exploit that potential as we could show. Many further research works are currently going on that will be of relevance, too.

Another interesting issue is the integration of semantic mechanisms and the adoption of ontology engineering. One limitation of CorA is that so far we did not focus on modeling the knowledge of the domain, which in our case was emergency management. Ontologies could be exploited to increase interoperability a priori, which again is a matter of better resolving interdependencies (i.e., coordination). Further research work will have to be invested in finding ways to prepare CorA such that ontologies (based on the respective application area) can be easily integrated.

For a rather long-term vision[1] a major challenge of future information systems will be the coordination of *knowledge*. Hence, a further very interesting extension to CorA—as a sub-philosophical domain of ontology—would be *doxastic* considerations [23,176]. Doxastic is the logic of reasoning about believes. Every knowledge source is tagged—e.g., according to its trustworthiness. Due to the fact that there is no absolute knowledge, contradicting knowledge is not possible. Merely contradicting beliefs or views are possible and it is up to the requester how to deal with it. This approach can address data inconsistency, which due to the characteristics of pervasive environments such as frequent unavailability is a common state, better than conventional, epistemic mechanisms. In fact, this is a quite "natural" way of dealing with inconsistent interdependencies. Human beings act similarly when information is exchanged. First of all we know what we know and this is usually trustworthy. If we get contradicting information from various sources we judge on the basis of the trustworthiness of the respective source. This is basically what the doxastic idea is about. This is a field that seams to be reasonable and should be explored further as it seems to have the potential to be exploited for improving coordination systems such as CorA further.

For the investigations carried out and presented in this book, we conclude that by explicitly respecting the concept of coordination we can exploit an optimisation potential. We claim this is true not only for the presented showcase of collaborating mobile users but on a general perspective. To put it into a nutshell: one efficient approach to solve a problem or improve a process is to identify the occurring interdependencies and try to resolve them as economically as possible. In other words this is *explicitly* dealing with *coordination* in order to *exploit an optimisation potential*.

---

[1] This was discovered and discussed in [22] during the IEEE Workshop on Coordination Models and Applications (CoMA): Knowledge in Pervasive Environments which was held at the WETICE conference in 2008.

Appendix

This section lists *definitions* that are used throughout the book. Some of the definitions are results of the presented research work (i.e., own definition), some were overtaken from literature, which is clearly indicated by citing the sources, and some were adapted from literature for the purpose of this work.

Defintion 1 (Collaboration). *Collaboration is the act of two or more parties—be those individuals or groups which may or may not have any previous relationship—doing something together towards a common goal to gain mutual benefit. The result is far superior to that which any party alone could ever produce.*

Defintion 2 (Computer Supported Cooperative Work CSCW [184]). *Computer Supported Cooperative Work (CSCW) is a generic term which combines the understanding of the way people work in groups with the enabling technologies of computer networking, and associated hardware, software, services and techniques.*

Defintion 3 (Coordination). *Coordination is the act of managing* interdependencies *between* actors *and* activities *by consideration of* constraints *for the purpose of achieving* goals.

Defintion 4 (Ubiquitous Computing [182]). *Ubiquitous computing is the method of enhancing computer use by making many computers available throughout the physical environment, but making them effectively invisible to the user.*

Defintion 5 (Pervasive Computing [79]). *Pervasive computing describes the convenient access, through a new class of appliances, to relevant information with the ability to easily take action on it when and where you need it.*

Defintion 6 (Coordination Law (adapted from [40])). *Coordination laws describe mechnisms that can be applied to resolve interdependencies occuring in coordination problems.*

Defintion 7 (Coordinable (adapted from [40])). *A coordinable is the subject of coordination that needs to be coordinated in coordination problems.*

Defintion 8 (Coordination Medium (adapted from [40])). *The coordination medium represents communication means, which serve as connectors between coordinables and facilitate communication.*

Defintion 9 (Software Agent [185]). *An agent is an encapsulated computer system that is situated in some environment, and that is capable of flexible, autonomous action in that environment in order to meet its design objectives.*

Defintion 10 (Peer-to-Peer Network [21]). *A peer-to-peer network refers to a distributed network of interconnected, heterogeneous entities (peers) which are able to dynamically adapt to the topology of the overlay network* defined by the available nodes, for the purpose to of exploiting shared resources respectively distributed information independent from any central authority, where communication is conducted in an equal way among equal nodes; where each node has an equal right to transiently adopt a certain role

Defintion 11 (Tuple Space, adapted from [69]). *A tuple space is a shared object space, that can be distributed over more nodes, where processes can have access to. Shared objects (i.e., tuples) can be put into the space, removed from the space or just read, which implies that they remain in the space.*

Defintion 12 (Tuple, adapted from [69]). *A tuple is the data item (i.e., a shared object) that is placed into, removed from, or read from a tuple space. It is the subject of the data-oriented communication embodied by the tuple space paradigm.*

Defintion 13 (Coordination Language, adapted from [72]). *A coordination language is the concrete implementation ("linguistic embodiment") of a coordination model with defined programming interfaces.*

Defintion 14 (Coordination Pattern, adapted from [66]). *A coordination pattern is a three-part rule that proposes a generic solution to a coordination problem as a relation between a certain context, a certain system of forces that occurs repeatedly in that context, and a certain configuration of coodinables, interdependencies and coordination laws that allows these forces to resolve themselves.*

Defintion 15 (Pattern Language [44]). *A pattern language is a structured collection of patterns that build on each other to transform needs and constraints into an architecture.*

Defintion 16 (GeoCollaboration [15]). *GeoCollaboration denotes any collaborative activity supported through the use of geo-information technologies.*

Bibliography

[1] G. D. Abowd, A. K. Dey, P. J. Brown, N. Davies, M. Smith, and P. Steggles. Towards a better understanding of context and context-awareness. In *HUC '99: Proceedings of the 1st International Symposium on Handheld and Ubiquitous Computing*, pages 304–307, London, UK, 1999. Springer-Verlag.

[2] C. Alexander. *The Timeless Way of Building*. Oxford University Press, 1979.

[3] S. Androutsellis-Theotokis and D. Spinellis. A survey of peer-to-peer content distribution technologies. *ACM Comput. Surv.*, 36(4):335–371, 2004.

[4] A. I. Antón and C. Potts. The use of goals to surface requirements for evolving systems. In *ICSE '98: Proceedings of the 20th International Conference on Software Engineering*, pages 157–166, Washington, DC, USA, 1998. IEEE Computer Society.

[5] Y. Aridor and D. B. Lange. Agent design patterns: elements of agent application design. In *AGENTS '98: Proceedings of the Second International Conference on Autonomous Agents*, pages 108–115. ACM, 1998.

[6] K. Arrow. *Social Choice and Individual Values*. John Wiley & Sons, 1951.

[7] J. H. Bair. Supporting cooperative work with computers: Addressing meeting mania. In *34th IEEE Computer Society International Conference–CompCon*, pages 208–217, 1989.

[8] A.-L. Barabasi and E. Bonabeau. Scale-free networks. *Scientific American*, 288:60–69, May 2003.

[9] K. Beck and R. Johnson. Patterns generate architectures. *Lecture Notes in Computer Science*, 821:139–149, 1994.

[10] K. Birman and T. Joseph. Exploiting virtual synchrony in distributed systems. *SIGOPS Oper. Syst. Rev.*, 21(5):123–138, 1987.

[11] G. Blair, N. Davies, A. Friday, and S. Wade. Quality of service support in a mobile environment: An approach based on tuple spaces. In *Proceedings 5th International Workshop on Quality of Service (IWQOS'97)*, pages 37–48, Columbia University, New York, USA, 1997.

[12] U. M. Borghoff and J. H. Schlichter. *Computer-Supported Cooperative Work: Introduction to Distributed Applications*. Springer, 2000.

[13] M. Bortenschlager. A flexible coordination language for pervasive computing environments. In T. P. et al., editor, *Advances in Pervasive Computing. Adjunct Proceedings of the 4th International Conference on Pervasive Computing*, Dublin, 2006.

[14] M. Bortenschlager, G. Castelli, A. Rosi, and F. Zambonelli. A context-sensitive infrastructure for coordinating agents in ubiquitous environments. *Special Issue on Engineering Environments for Multiagent Systems of International Journal on Multiagent and Grid Systems*, 2008.

[15] M. Bortenschlager, T. Fichtel, S. Leitinger, H. Rieser, and R. Steinmann. A map- and location-based geocollaboration system for disaster management in outdoor environments. In *4th International Symposium on LBS and TeleCartography*, Hong Kong, 2007.

[16] M. Bortenschlager, N. Göll, E. Haid, H. Rieser, and R. Steinmann. Geocollaboration – location-based collaboration in emergency scenarios. In *The 17th IEEE International Workshops on Enabling Technologies: Infrastructure for Collaborative Enterprises (WETICE): Workshop on Coordination Models and Applications (CoMA): Knowledge in Pervasive Environments*, Rome, Italy, 2008.

[17] M. Bortenschlager, G. Kotsis, and M. Mamei. Current developments and future challenges of coordination in pervasive environments. In *The 16th IEEE International Workshops on Enabling Technologies: Infrastructure for Collaborative Enterprises (WETICE): Workshop on Interdisciplinary Aspects of Coordination Applied to Pervasive Environments: Models and Applications (CoMA)*, Paris, 2007.

[18] M. Bortenschlager, G. Kotsis, and M. Mamei. Towards a coordination framework for pervasive environments. *Ubiquitous Computing and Communication Journal*, 3:1–7, 2008.

[19] M. Bortenschlager, G. Kotsis, and S. Reich. A generic coordination architecture as an enabler for mobile collaborative applications. In *Distributed and Mobile Collaboration (DMC 2006) Workshop - WETICE, Manchester, UK*, 2006.

[20] M. Bortenschlager, G. Kotsis, and S. Reich. An architectural approach to apply the supervisor/worker collaboration pattern to nomadic workspaces. In *The 16th IEEE International Workshops on Enabling Technologies: Infrastructure for Collaborative Enterprises (WETICE). Distributed and Mobile Collaboration Workshop*, Paris, 2007.

[21] M. Bortenschlager, S. Leitinger, H. Rieser, and R. Steinmann. Towards a p2p-based geocollaboration system for disaster management. In *GI-Days*, Münster, Germany, 2007.

[22] M. Bortenschlager, L. Nixon, E. Simperl, and R. Tolksdorf. Coordination of knowledge in pervasive environments. In *The 17th IEEE International Workshops on Enabling Technologies: Infrastructure for Collaborative Enterprises (WETICE): Workshop on Coordination Models and Applications (CoMA): Knowledge in Pervasive Environments*, Rome, Italy, 2008.

[23] M. Bortenschlager, H. Rieser, B. Salvatore, R. Steinmann, J. Strobl, and G. Vetere. Ontology-based geodata integration for emergency management systems. In *Geoinformatics Forum*, Salzburg, Austria, 2008.

[24] M. Bratman. *Intention, Plans, and Practical Reason*. CSLI Publications, 1999.

[25] F. P. Brooks, editor. *The Mythical Man-Month: Essays on Software Engineering*. Addison-Wesley Professional, 1995.

[26] R. A. Brooks. A robot that walks; emergent behaviors from a carefully evolved network. Technical report, Massachusetts Institute of Technology, Cambridge, MA, USA, 1989.

[27] F. Buschmann, R. Meunier, H. Rohnert, P. Sommerlad, and M. Stal. *Pattern-Oriented Software Architecture: A System of Pattern*. John Wiley, 1996.

[28] V. Bush. As we may think. *Atlantic Monthly*, 176:101–108, 1945.

[29] N. Busi, R. Gorrieri, and G. Zavattaro. A process algebraic view of linda coordination primitives. *Theor. Comput. Sci.*, 192(2):167–199, 1998.

[30] S. Bussmann and J. Mueller. A negotiation framework for cooperating agents. In S. M. Deen, editor, *CKBS-SIG: Proc. of the Special Interest Group on Cooperating Knowledge Based Systems (1992)*, pages 1–17. DAKE Centre, Keele, 1993.

[31] G. Cabri, L. Leonardi, and F. Zambonelli. Reactive tuple spaces for mobile agent coordination. In *MA '98: Proceedings of the Second International Workshop on Mobile Agents*, pages 237–248. Springer-Verlag, 1999.

[32] G. Cabri, L. Leonardi, and F. Zambonelli. Mars: A programmable coordination architecture for mobile agents. *IEEE Internet Computing*, 4(4):26–35, 2000.

[33] B. Carbunar, M. T. Valente, and J. Vitek. Coordination and mobility in corelime. *Mathematical. Structures in Comp. Sci.*, 14(3):397–419, 2004.

[34] N. Carriero and D. Gelernter. A computational model of everything. *Commun. ACM*, 44(11):77–81, 2001.

[35] J. M. Carroll. *Scenario-Based Design: Envisioning Work and Technology in System Development*. John Wiley & Sons, 1995.

[36] G. Castelli, A. Rosi, M. Mamei, and F. Zambonelli. A simple model and infrastructure for context-aware browsing of the world. In *PERCOM '07: Proceedings of the Fifth IEEE International Conference on Pervasive Computing and Communications*, pages 229–238, Washington, DC, USA, 2007. IEEE Computer Society.

[37] K. Chandy and J. Misra. *Parallel Program Design: A Foundation*. Addison-Wesley, 1988.

[38] X. Chang and S. C. Cheung. Inconsistency detection and resolution for context-aware middleware support. In *4th International ACM Symposium on the Foundations of Software Engineering,*, Lisbon, Portugal, 2005.

[39] G. Chen and D. Kotz. A survey of context-aware mobile computing research. Technical Report Technical Report TR2000-381, Dept. of Computer Science, Dartmouth College, 2000.

[40] P. Ciancarini. Coordination models and languages as software integrators. *ACM Comput. Surv.*, 28(2):300–302, 1996.

[41] L. Clausen, E. M. Geenen, and E. Macamo. *Entsetzliche soziale Prozesse. Theoretische und empirische Annäherungen.* Lit-Verlag, 2003.

[42] A. Cockburn, editor. *Agile Software Development.* Addison-Wesley Professional, 2001.

[43] J. O. Coplien. *Advanced C++ Programming Styles and Idioms.* Addison-Wesley, 1991.

[44] J. O. Coplien. Software design patterns: common questions and answers. In *The patterns handbooks: techniques, strategies, and applications*, pages 311–319. Cambridge University Press, New York, NY, USA, 1998.

[45] P. Costa, L. Mottola, A. L. Murphy, and G. P. Picco. Programming wireless sensor networks with the teenylime middleware. In *Proceedings of the 8th ACM/IFIP/USENIX International Middleware Conference (Middleware 2007)*, Newport Beach (CA, USA), November 2007.

[46] C. Curino, M. Giani, M. Giorgetta, A. Giusti, A. L. Murphy, and G. P. Picco. Mobile data collection in sensor networks: The TINYLIME middleware. *Elsevier Pervasive and Mobile Computing Journal*, 4(1):446–469, Dec. 2005.

[47] S. B. Davidson, H. Garcia-Molina, and D. Skeen. Consistency in a partitioned network: a survey. *ACM Comput. Surv.*, 17(3):341–370, 1985.

[48] R. de Freitas Bulcao Neto and M. da Graca Campos Pimentel. Toward a domain-independent semantic model for context-aware computing. In *LA-WEB '05: Proceedings of the Third Latin American Web Congress*, page 61, Washington, DC, USA, 2005. IEEE Computer Society.

[49] G. de Giacomo, Y. Lespérance, and H. J. Levesque. Congolog, a concurrent programming language based on the situation calculus. *Artif. Intell.*, 121(1-2):109–169, 2000.

[50] M. de Leoni, M. Mecella, and G. D. Giacomo. Highly dynamic adaptation in process management systems through execution monitoring. In *Business Process Management*, pages 182–197, 2007.

[51] M. de Leoni, M. Mecella, F. D. Rosa, A. Marrella, A. Poggi, A. Krek, and F. Manti. Emergency management: from user requirements to a flexible p2p architecture. In *4th International Conference on Information Systems for Crisis Response and Management (ISCRAM)*, Delft, the Netherlands, 2007.

[52] H. DeMeer and C. Koppen. Self-organisation in peer-to-peer systems. In R. Steinmetz and K. Wehrle, editors, *Peer-to-Peer Systems and Applications*, pages 247–268, 2005.

[53] R. DeNicola, G. Ferrari, and R. Pugliese. Klaim: A kernel language of agents interaction and mobility. *IEEE Trans. on Software Engineering*, 24(5), 1998.

[54] P. J. Denning. Hastily formed networks. *Commun. ACM*, 49(4):15–20, 2006.

[55] D. Deugo, M. Weiss, and E. Kendall. Reusable pattern for agent coordination. In A. Omicini, F. Zambonelli, M. Klusch, and R. Tolksdorf, editors, *Coordination of Internet Agents: Models, Technologies, and Applications*, pages 347–368. Springer, 2001.

[56] A. K. Dey, G. D. Abowd, and D. Salber. A context-based infrastructure for smart environments. In *1st International Workshop on Managing Interactions in Smart Environments (MANSE 99)*, pages 114–128, 1999.

[57] M. Dorigo, G. D. Caro, and T. Stuetzle. Special issue on ant algorithms. *Future Generation Computer Systems Journal*, 16(8):1–17, 2000.

[58] S. Dustdar and T. Hoffmann. Interaction pattern detection in process oriented information systems. *Data and Knowledge Engineering*, 62(1):138–155, 2007.

[59] A. Etzioni. *Modern Organizations.* Prentice-Hall, Englewood Cliffs, NJ, USA, 1964.

[60] D. Fensel. Triple-Space Computing: Semantic Web Services Based on Persistent Publication of Information. In F. A. Aagesen, C. Anutariya, and V. Wuwongse, editors, *Proc. of the IFIP Int'l Conf. on Intelligence in Communication Systems*, volume 3283 of *Lecture Notes in Computer Science*, pages 43–53. Springer-Verlag, 2004.

[61] A. Ferscha. Coordination in pervasive computing environments. In *Proceedings of the 12th IEEE International Workshops on Enabling Technologies: Infrastructure for Collaborative Enterprises (WETICE-2003)*. IEEE Computer Society Press, June 2003.

[62] A. Ferscha and C. Scheiner. Collective choice in virtual teams. In *Proceedings of the 8th International Workshops on Enabling Technologies: Infrastructures for Collaborative Enterprises (WETICE 1999)*, pages 96–101, Stanford, CA, USA, June 1999. IEEE CS Press.

[63] C.-L. Fok, G.-C. Roman, and G. Hackmann. A lightweight coordination middleware for mobile computing. In *Coordination Models and Languages, 6th International Conference (COORDINATION)*, pages 135–151, 2004.

[64] E. Freeman, S. Hupfer, and K. Arnold. *JavaSpaces Principles, Patterns, and Practice*. Pearson Education, 1999.

[65] D. Fudenberg and J. Tirole. *Game Theory*. MIT Press, 1991.

[66] R. Gabriel. A timeless way of hacking. In J. Crupi, D. Alur, and D. Malks, editors, *Core J2EE Patterns. Best Practices and Strategies*. Prentice Hall, 2001.

[67] E. Gamma, R. Helm, R. Johnson, and J. Vlissides. *Design Patterns: Elements of Reusable Object-Oriented Software*. Addison-Wesley Professional, 1995.

[68] E. Gams and S. Reich. An analysis of the applicability of user trails in web applications. *Journal of Web Engineering*, 5(3), 2006.

[69] D. Gelernter. Generative communication in linda. *ACM Trans. Program. Lang. Syst.*, 7(1):80–112, 1985.

[70] D. Gelernter. Multiple tuple spaces in linda. In *PARLE '89: Proceedings of the Parallel Architectures and Languages Europe, Volume II: Parallel Languages*, pages 20–27, London, UK, 1989. Springer-Verlag.

[71] D. Gelernter and A. J. Bernstein. Distributed communication via global buffer. In *PODC '82: Proceedings of the first ACM SIGACT-SIGOPS symposium on Principles of distributed computing*, pages 10–18. ACM Press, 1982.

[72] D. Gelernter and N. Carriero. Coordination languages and their significance. *Commun. ACM*, 35(2):96, 1992.

[73] N. Gershenfeld, R. Krikorian, and D. Cohen. The internet of things. *Scientific American*, 291(4):76–81, October 2004.

[74] P.-P. Grasse. La reconstruction du nid et les coordinations inter-individuelles chez bellicositermes natalensis et cubitermes sp. la thorie de la stigmergie: Essai d'interprtation du comportement des termites constructeurs. *Insectes Sociaux*, 6:41–83, 1959.

[75] J. Gray, P. Helland, P. O'Neil, and D. Shasha. The dangers of replication and a solution. In *SIGMOD '96: Proceedings of the 1996 ACM SIGMOD International Conference on Management of Data*, pages 173–182, New York, NY, USA, 1996. ACM.

[76] R. Greene. *Confronting Catastrophe: A GIS Handbook*. ESRI Press, 2002.

[77] J. Grudin. Computer-supported cooperative work: History and focus. *Computer*, 27(5):19–26, 1994.

[78] P. H. Gulliver. *Disputes and Negotiations - A Cross-cultural Perspective*. Academic Press, 1997.

[79] U. Hansmann, L. Merk, M. S. Nicklous, and T. Stober. *Pervasive Computing Handbook*. Springer-Verlag Berlin, 2001.

[80] P. Haumer, M. Jarke, , K. Pohl, and P. Heymans. Bridging the gap between past and future in re: A scenario-based approach. In *IEEE International Symposium on Requirements Engineering*, pages 66–73, Los Alamitos, CA, USA, 1999. IEEE Computer Society.

[81] K. Henricksen, J. Indulska, and A. Rakotonirainy. Developing context-aware pervasive computing applications: Models and approach. *Pervasive and Mobile Computing*, 2(1):37–64, 2006.

[82] C. A. R. Hoare. An axiomatic basis for computer programming. *Commun. ACM*, 12(10):576–580, 1969.

[83] O. Holland and C. Melhuish. Stigmergy, self-organization, and sorting in collective robotics. *Artif. Life*, 5(2):173–202, 1999.

[84] S. R. Humayoun, T. Catarci, M. de Leoni, A. Marrella, M. Mecella, M. Bortenschlager, and R. Steinmann. Designing mobile systems in highly dynamic scenarios. the workpad methodology. *Journal on Knowledge, Technology, and Policy*, 22(1), 2009.

[85] S. R. Humayoun, T. Catarci, M. de Leoni, A. Marrella, M. Mecella, M. Bortenschlager, and R. Steinmann. The workpad user interface and methodology: Developing smart and effective mobile applications for emergency operators. In *HCI International 2009*, San Diego, CA, USA, 2009.

[86] K. A. Hummel. Mobility aware adaptation of space based coordination patterns. *Ingénierie des Systèmes d'Information*, 9(2):87–106, 2004.

[87] S. C. Hupfer. Melinda: Linda with multiple tuple space. Technical Report Technical Report YALE/DCS/RR-766, Yale University, 1990.

[88] W. Jäger. *Aristotle's Metaphysica*. Oxford University Press, 1957.

[89] P. Jalote. *Fault Tolerance in Distributed Systems*. Prentice Hall, 1994.

[90] N. R. Jennings. Commitments and conventions: The foundation of coordination in multi-agent systems. *The Knowledge Engineering Review*, 8(3):223–250, 1993.

[91] N. R. Jennings. Coordination techniques for distributed artificial intelligence. In O. G. M. P. and J. N. R., editors, *Foundations of Distributed Artificial Intelligence*, pages 187–210. Wiley, 1993.

[92] N. R. Jennings. Agent-based computing: Promise and perils. In *Proc. 16th Int. Joint Conf. on Artificial Intelligence (IJCAI-99)*, pages 1429–1436, 1999.

[93] N. R. Jennings, T. J. Norman, P. Faratin, P. O'Brien, and B. Odgers. Autonomous agents for business process management. *Int. Journal of Applied Artificial Intelligence*, 14(2):145–189, 2000.

[94] B. Johanson and A. Fox. The event heap: A coordination infrastructure for interactive workspaces. In *WMCSA*, pages 83–93, 2002.

[95] B. Johanson, T. Winograd, and A. Fox. Interactive workspaces. *Computer*, 36(4):99–101, 2003.

[96] C. Julien and G.-C. Roman. Egospaces: Facilitating rapid development of context-aware mobile applications. *IEEE Transactions on Software Engineering*, 32(5):281–298, May 2006.

[97] W. Kellerer, R. Schollmeier, and K. Wehrle. Peer-to-peer in mobile environments. In R. Steinmetz and K. Wehrle, editors, *Peer-to-Peer Systems and Applications*, pages 401–417, 2005.

[98] E. A. Kendall, P. V. M. Krishna, C. V. Pathak, and C. B. Suresh. Patterns of intelligent and mobile agents. In *AGENTS '98: Proceedings of the Second International Conference on Autonomous Agents*, pages 92–99. ACM, 1998.

[99] T. Kindberg and A. Fox. System software for ubiquitous computing. *IEEE Pervasive Computing*, 1(1):70–81, 2002.

[100] M. Klein. Coordination science: Challenges and directions. In *Coordination Technology for Collaborative Applications*, pages 161–176, 1996.

[101] L. Kleinrock. On some principles of nomadic computing and multi-access communications. *Communications Magazine*, 38(7):46–50, 2000.

[102] Kühn, e., Beinhart, M., and Murth, M. Improving data quality of mobile internet applications with an extensible virtual shared memory approach. In *IADIS WWW/Internet 2005 Conference*, 2005.

[103] T. J. Lehman, S. W. McLaughry, and P. Wyckoff. T spaces: The next wave. In *HICSS*, 1999.

[104] S. Leitinger. Comparision of gis-based public safety systems for emergency management. In *24th Urban Data Management Symposium, UDMS*, 2004.

[105] K. Lewin. *A dynamic theory of personality*. McGraw-Hill, 1935.

[106] P. Maes. Agents that reduce work and information overload. *Communications of the ACM*, 37(7):31–40, 1994.

[107] P. Maes. Pattie maes on software agents: Humanizing the global computer. *IEEE Internet Computing*, 1(4):10–19, 1997.

[108] Q. H. Mahmoud and L. Yu. Making software agents user-friendly. *Computer*, 39(7):96–95, 2006.

[109] T. W. Malone and K. Crowston. The interdisciplinary study of coordination. *ACM Comput. Surv.*, 26(1):87–119, 1994.

[110] M. Mamei and F. Zambonelli. Field-based approaches to adaptive motion coordination in pervasive computing scenarios. In *Handbook of Algorithms for Mobile and Wireless Networking and Computing*. CRC Press, 2004.

[111] M. Mamei and F. Zambonelli. Programming pervasive and mobile computing applications with the tota middleware. In *PERCOM '04: Proceedings of the Second IEEE International Conference on Pervasive Computing and Communications (PerCom'04)*, page 263, Washington, DC, USA, 2004. IEEE Computer Society.

[112] C. Mascolo, L. Capra, and W. Emmerich. Mobile computing middleware. In *Advanced Lectures on Networking*, pages 20–58. Springer-Verlag, 2002.

[113] F. Mattern and P. Sturm. From distributed systems to ubiquitous computing – the state of the art, trends, and prospects of future networked systems. In K. Irmscher and K.-P. Fähnrich, editors, *Proc. KIVS 2003*, pages 3–25, Springer-Verlag, Feb. 2003.

[114] P. J. McCann and G.-C. Roman. Compositional programming abstractions for mobile computing. *Software Engineering*, 24(2):97–110, 1998.

[115] M. Mecella, T. Catarci, M. Angelaccio, B. Buttarazzi, A. Krek, S. Dustdar, and G. Vetere. Workpad: 2-layered peer-to-peer for emergency management through adaptive processes. In *CollaborateCom*, Atlanta, Georgia, USA, 2006.

[116] S. Milgram. The small world problem. *Psychology Today*, pages 60–67, May 1967.

[117] R. Milner. *Communication and concurrency*. Prentice-Hall, Inc., Upper Saddle River, NJ, USA, 1989.

[118] R. Milner. *Communicating and Mobile Systems: the Pi-Calculus*. Cambridge Univ. Press, 1999.

[119] R. Milner, J. Parrow, and D. Walker. A calculus of mobile processes. *Information and Computation*, 100:1–40, 1992.

[120] G. Mühl, A. Ulbrich, K. Herrmann, and T. Weis. Disseminating information to mobile clients using publish-subscribe. *IEEE Internet Computing*, 8(3):46–53, 2004.

[121] A. L. Murphy and G. P. Picco. Using LIME to support replication for availability in mobile ad hoc networks. In *Proceedings of the 8th International Conference on Coordination Models and Languages (COORD06)*, Lecture Notes on Computer Science, Bologna (Italy), June 2006. Springer.

[122] A. L. Murphy, G. P. Picco, and G.-C. Roman. Lime: A middleware for physical and logical mobility. In F. Golshani, P. Dasgupta, and W. Zhao, editors, *Proceedings of the 21st International Conference on Distributed Computing Systems (ICDCS-21)*, Phoenix, AZ, USA), 2001.

[123] A. L. Murphy, G. P. Picco, and G.-C. Roman. LIME: A coordination model and middleware supporting mobility of hosts and agents. *ACM Transactions on Software Engineering and Methodology (TOSEM)*, 15(3):279–328, 2006.

[124] J. Nash. Equilibrium points in n-person games. In *Proceedings of the National Academy of Sciences*, volume 36, pages 48–49, 1950.

[125] B. C. Neuman. Scale in distributed systems. In *Readings in Distributed Computing Systems*, pages 463–489. IEEE Computer Society Press, 1994.

[126] A. Newell and H. Simon. *Human problem solving*. Prentice-Hall, Englewood Cliffs, NJ, USA, 1972.

[127] J. Nielsen. *Usability Engineering*. Academic Press, 1993.

[128] H. P. Nii. Blackboard systems. In B. et al., editor, *The Handbook of Artificial Intelligence*, pages 1–82. Addison-Wesley, Reading, MA, USA, 2004.

[129] H. Nurmi. Voting procedures: A summary analysis. *British Journal of Political Science*, 13(2):181–208, 1983.

[130] H. S. Nwana, L. Lee, and N. R. Jennings. Coordination in software agent systems. *The British Telecom Technical Journal*, 14(4):79–88, 1996.

[131] C. Obermair, B. Ploderer, W. Reitberger, and M. Tscheligi. Cues in the environment: a design principle for ambient intelligence. In *CHI '06 Extended Abstracts on Human Factors in Computing Systems*, pages 1157–1162, New York, NY, USA, 2006. ACM Press.

[132] A. Omicini, A. Ricci, and M. Viroli. *Agens Faber*: Toward a theory of artefacts for MAS. *Electronic Notes in Theoretical Computer Sciences*, 150(3):21–36, 29 May 2006. 1st International Workshop on Coordination and Organization (CoOrg 2005), COORDINATION 2005.

[133] A. Omicini and F. Zambonelli. Tuple centres for the coordination of internet agents. In *SAC '99: Proceedings of the 1999 ACM Symposium on Applied Computing*, pages 183–190, New York, NY, USA, 1999. ACM Press.

[134] D. S. Parker, G. J. Popek, G. Rudisin, A. Stoughton, B. J. Walker, E. Walton, J. M. Chow, D. A. Edwards, S. Kiser, and C. S. Kline. Detection of mutual inconsistency in distributed systems. *IEEE Transactions on Software Engineering*, 9(3):240–247, 1983.

[135] A. Paschke, C. Kiss, and S. Al-Hunaty. Npl: Negotiation pattern language - a design pattern language for decentralized (agent) coordination and negotiation protocols. In R. Banda, editor, *E-Negotiation - An Introduction*. ICFAI University Press, 2006.

[136] J. Payton, G.-C. Roman, and C. Julien. Context-sensitive data structures supporting software development in ad hoc mobile settings. In *Proceedings of the 3rd International Workshop on Software Engineering for Large-Scale Multi-Agent Systems, co-located with ICSE 2004*, pages 34–41, May 2004.

[137] G. P. Picco, D. Balzarotti, and P. Costa. LIGHTS: A lightweight, customizable tuple space supporting context-aware applications. In *Proceedings of the 20th ACM Symposium on Applied Computing (SAC05)*, Santa Fe (New Mexico, USA), Mar. 2005. ACM Press.

[138] G. P. Picco, A. L. Murphy, and G.-C. Roman. LIME: Linda meets mobility. In D. Garlan, editor, *Proceedings of the 21st International Conference on Software Engineering (ICSE'99)*, pages 368–377, Los Angeles, CA, USA, May 1999. ACM Press. Also available as Technical Report WUCS-98-21, July 1998, Washington University in St. Louis, MO, USA.

[139] G. P. Picco, G.-C. Roman, and P. J. McCann. Reasoning about code mobility with mobile UNITY. *ACM Transactions on Software Engineering and Methodology (TOSEM)*, 10(3):338–395, 2001.

[140] A. S. Rao and M. P. Georgeff. BDI-agents: from theory to practice. In *Proceedings of the First Intl. Conference on Multiagent Systems*, San Francisco, 1995.

[141] B. Rhodes, N. Minar, and J. Weaver. Wearable computing meets ubiquitous computing: Reaping the best of both worlds. In *The Third International Symposium on Wearable Computers (ISWC '99)*, pages 141–149, 1999.

[142] G.-C. Roman and P. J. McCann. An introduction to mobile UNITY. In *IPPS/SPDP Workshops*, pages 871–880, 1998.

[143] G.-C. Roman, P. J. McCann, and J. Y. Plun. Mobile unity: reasoning and specification in mobile computing. *ACM Trans. Softw. Eng. Methodol.*, 6(3):250–282, 1997.

[144] D. Rosenblum. Some open problems in publish/subscribe networking, 2003.

[145] A. I. T. Rowstron and A. Wood. Solving the linda multiple rd problem. In *COORDINATION '96: Proceedings of the First International Conference on Coordination Languages and Models*, pages 357–367. Springer-Verlag, 1996.

[146] M. Satyanarayanan. Pervasive computing: Vision and challenges. *IEEE Personal Communications*, pages 10–17, Aug. 2001.

[147] K. Schelfthout, T. Holvoet, and Y. Berbers. Views: Customizable abstractions for contextaware applications in manets. In *SELMAS '05: Proceedings of the Fourth International Workshop on Software Engineering for Large-scale Multi-agent Systems*, pages 1–8. ACM Press, 2005.

[148] K. Schelfthout, D. Weyns, and T. Holvoet. Middleware for protocol-based coordination in mobile applications. *IEEE Distributed Systems Online*, 7(8):1–18, Aug. 2006. ISSN = 1541-4922.

[149] T. C. Schelling. *Strategy of Conflict*. Harvard University Press, 1960.

[150] B. N. Schilit. *A system architecture for context-aware mobile computing*. PhD thesis, Columbia University, 1995.

[151] B. N. Schilit, N. Adams, and R. Want. Context-aware computing applications. In *1st Workshop on Mobile Computing Systems and Applications*, Lake District, UK, 1994.

[152] A. Schmidt. *Ubiquitous Computing – Computing in Context*. PhD thesis, Lancaster University, 2002.

[153] A. Schmidt, K. A. Aidoo, A. Takaluoma, U. Tuomela, K. V. Laerhoven, and W. V. de Velde. Advanced interaction in context. In *International Symposium on Handheld and Ubiquitous Computing*, Karlsruhe, Germany, 1999.

[154] A. Schmidt, M. Beigl, and H. w. Gellersen. There is more to context than location. *Computers and Graphics*, 23:893–901, 1999.

[155] F. Schmuck. *Picking the cheapest broadcast protocols in a distributed program*. PhD thesis, Cornell Univ. Dept. of Computer Science, 1987.

[156] A. K. Sen. *Collective Choice and Social Welfare*. Elsevier Science, 1984.

[157] J. M. Shell. Understand and implement the message bus pattern, 2004. IBM, December.
[158] C. Sierra, P. Faratin, and N. R. Jennings. A service-oriented negotiation model between autonomous agents. In *Proc. of the Eighth European Workshop on Modeling Autonomous Agents in a Multi-Agent World (MAAMAW-97)*, pages 17–35, 1997.
[159] B. Singh. Invited talk on coordination systems, 1989. Organizational Computing Conference, November 13-14, Austin, Texas.
[160] R. G. Smith. The contract net protocol: High-level communication and control in a distributed problem solver. In A. H. Bond and L. Gasser, editors, *Readings in Distributed Artificial Intelligence*, pages 357–366. Kaufmann, San Mateo, CA, 1988.
[161] M. E. Sorrows and S. C. Hirtle. The nature of landmarks for real and electronic spaces. In C. Freksa and D. M. Mark, editors, *Spatial Information Theory: Cognitive and Computational Foundations of Geographic Information Science, International Conference COSIT '99*, volume 1661 of *Lecture Notes in Computer Science*, pages 37–50, 1999.
[162] T. Strang, C. Linnhoff-Popien, and K. Frank. Cool: A context ontology language to enable contextual interoperability. In *Proceedings of 4th IFIP WG 6.1 International Conference on Distributed Applications and Interoperable Systems (DAIS2003)*, pages 236–247, Paris/France, 2003. Springer Verlag.
[163] J. Surowiecki. *The Wisdom of Crowds*. Anchor, 2005.
[164] A. Sutcliffe. Scenario-based requirements engineering. In *RE '03: Proceedings of the 11th IEEE International Conference on Requirements Engineering*, Washington, DC, USA, 2003. IEEE Computer Society.
[165] A. G. Sutcliffe, N. A. Maiden, S. Minocha, and D. Manuel. Supporting scenario-based requirements engineering. *IEEE Transactions on Software Engineering*, 24(12):1072–1088, 1998.
[166] A. S. Tanenbaum and M. van Steen. *Distributed Systems: Principles and Paradims*. Prentice Hall, 2002.
[167] G. Technologies. Gigaspaces platform, 2002. Retrieved on 3 November 2008 from http://www.techieindex.net/whitepapers/pdf/GigaSpacesWhitePaper.pdf.
[168] S. Teufel, C. Sauter, T. Mühlherr, and K. Bauknecht. *Computerunterstützung für die Gruppenarbeit*. Addison-Wesley, 1995.
[169] E. O. Thorp. The invention of the first wearable computer. In *The Second International Symposium on Wearable Computers*, pages 4–8. IEEE Computer Society, 1998.
[170] R. Tolksdorf. Coordination patterns in mobile object spaces. In *7th IEEE Workshops on Enabling Technologies: Infrastructures for Collaborative Enterprises*, pages 126–131. IEEE Computer Society Press, 1998.
[171] R. Tolksdorf, E. P. Bontas, and L. J. B. Nixon. Towards a tuplespace-based middleware for the semantic web. In *WI '05: Proceedings of the 2005 IEEE/WIC/ACM International Conference on Web Intelligence*, pages 338–344, Washington, DC, USA, 2005. IEEE Computer Society.
[172] R. Tolksdorf and D. Glaubitz. Coordinating web-based systems with documents in xmlspaces. In *CoopIS '01: Proceedings of the 9th International Conference on Cooperative Information Systems*, pages 356–370, London, UK, 2001. Springer-Verlag.
[173] R. Tolksdorf, L. Nixon, F. Liebsch, D. M. Nguyen, and E. P. Bontas. Semantic web spaces. Technical Report Technical Report TR-B-04-11, Freie Universität Berlin, Germany, 2004.
[174] D. Ungerer. Simple speech: Improving communication in disaster relief operations. In R. Dietrich and K. Jochum, editors, *Teaming Up: Components of Safety under High Risk*, pages 81–92. Aldershot: Ashgate, 2004.
[175] W. M. P. van der Aalst, A. H. M. ter Hofstede, B. Kiepuszewski, and A. P. Barros. Workflow patterns. *Distrib. Parallel Databases*, 14(1):5–51, 2003.
[176] G. Vetere, F. Venditti, and A. Faraotti. Semantic integration of peer to peer systems: A doxastic approach. In *International Conference on Semantic Computing*, pages 284–290, Los Alamitos, CA, USA, 2008. IEEE Computer Society.
[177] R. A. Virzi. Refining the test phase of usability evaluation: how many subjects is enough? *Hum. Factors*, 34(4):457–468, 1992.
[178] J. von Neumann and O. Morgenstern. *Theory of games and economic behavior*. Princeton University Press, 1944.

[179] S. P. Wade. *An Investigation into the use of the Tuple Space Paradigm in Mobile Computing Environments*. PhD thesis, Lancaster University, 1999.

[180] S. Wasserman and K. Faust. *Social Network Analysis: Methods and Applications*. Cambridge University Press, 1994.

[181] M. Weiser. The computer for the 21st century. *Scientific American*, 265(3):66–75, Sept. 1991.

[182] M. Weiser. Some computer science issues in ubiquitous computing. *Commun. ACM*, 36(7):75–84, 1993.

[183] D. Weyns, A. Omicini, and J. Odell. Environment as a first class abstraction in multiagent systems. *Autonomous Agents and Multi-Agent Systems*, 14(1):5–30, 2007.

[184] P. Wilson. *Computer Supported Cooperative Work: An Introduction*. Kluwer Academic Pub, 1991.

[185] M. Wooldridge. Agent-based software engineering. *IEE Proc. of Software Engineering*, 144(1):26–37, Feb 1997.

[186] M. Wooldridge. *Introduction to Multiagent Systems*. John Wiley and Sons, 2002.

VDM Verlagsservicegesellschaft mbH

Die VDM Verlagsservicegesellschaft sucht für wissenschaftliche Verlage abgeschlossene und herausragende

Dissertationen, Habilitationen, Diplomarbeiten, Master Theses, Magisterarbeiten usw.

für die kostenlose Publikation als Fachbuch.

Sie verfügen über eine Arbeit, die hohen inhaltlichen und formalen Ansprüchen genügt, und haben Interesse an einer honorarvergüteten Publikation?

Dann senden Sie bitte erste Informationen über sich und Ihre Arbeit per Email an *info@vdm-vsg.de*.

Sie erhalten kurzfristig unser Feedback!

VDM Verlagsservicegesellschaft mbH
Dudweiler Landstr. 99
D - 66123 Saarbrücken
Telefon +49 681 3720 174
Fax   +49 681 3720 1749
www.vdm-vsg.de

Die VDM Verlagsservicegesellschaft mbH vertritt

Printed by Books on Demand GmbH, Norderstedt / Germany